PRESCRIPTION FOR READING:
TEACH THEM PHONICS

by

ERNEST H. CHRISTMAN, M.D.

Illustrations by
CATHERINE A. CHRISTMAN

THE TUTORIAL PRESS, INC.

1. Reading
2. Phonetics

ISBN O-912329-00-9 Paperback
ISBN 0-912329-01-7 Hard Cover
Library of Congress Catalog Card Number: 83-70696

The Tutorial Press, Inc.
711-A Encino Place, N.E.
Albuquerque, New Mexico 87102

Dedicated to my son, Ernest Daniel Christman, whose need to learn to read caused this book to be written.

Grateful acknowledgment is made to my daughter, Catherine Ann Christman, who served as both editor and illustrator.

INTRODUCTION

A Note from the Author

This book is designed for parents who wish to teach their own children to read. As a practicing ophthalmologist, I see many children who are brought to me to determine why they are poor readers. In the great majority of cases, the eye examination shows normal visual function. Eye abnormalities almost never prevent the development of good reading skills. It is not the eye that reads, but the mind. The eye is only nature's way of getting information into the mind. I believe that most reading problems are the result of inadequate teachers and/or teaching methods.

Recent scientific research has shown that the mind processes verbal information by the medium of sound. Different centers of the brain each handle specific aspects of the spoken word. The right half of the brain handles vowel sounds while the left half handles consonants. There are also designated areas of the brain that handle specific aspects of grammar such as the use of conjunctions, articles, and even the employment of the passive voice.

In all written languages that employ an alphabet, the symbols on the page represent sounds. The reader sees the symbols and converts them into sound equivalents. To be intelligible, these sounds must match remembered sounds in the reader's mind. No one would expect a child to understand a foreign language that he has never been exposed to. The sounds do not match anything in the child's memory.

Introduction

The same situation occurs when encountering new sound combinations in a child's own language. The child understands only those sounds that match his memory bank. Reading cannot achieve more than listening to spoken words can accomplish. If a child does not understand what he is hearing (e.g. a discussion on astronomy), that is not considered unusual. But if a child has trouble understanding what is written in reading books, concern is often expressed over his ability to read without considering that the material may be too difficult for his level of understanding or that the words used, when properly sounded, do not exist in his memory bank.

This book is based upon phonics. I realize that there is a debate among educators over the value of teaching reading with a phonic approach. Many educators state flatly that phonics is not a tool to be used in teaching reading. Other teachers say that phonics is merely peripheral in teaching reading. Still others state that English is not a phonic language, and there are so many exceptions to the rule system that the teaching of phonics is virtually an impossible task, one that is better left alone.

I believe that these problems concerning the use of phonics in the teaching of reading stem from a misunderstanding that comes from unfamiliarity with phonics. That English is 98 per cent phonic will be apparent to anyone who finishes this book. But a major problem with teaching reading via phonics is a lack of appreciation of the fact that different levels of phonic difficulty do exist. The following sentence is illustrative:

The cat goes around at night.

To someone who can read, this sentence is quite simple. However, there is a great deal of phonic difficulty contained within it. The **th** is a digraph, a sound that is composed of two letters but is entirely different from the sound of each of the letters. In addition, the **th** can be pronounced "hard" as in the word the, or "soft" as in the word with. In the word **cat**, the letter c has the sound of k and not the s sound that is found in the word city. In the word **goes**, the g is "hard" (note the different sounds of g in the words gem and got). The letter o in **goes** is pronounced long, the e is silent, and the s is pronounced as a z. In the word **around**, the a is not pronounced as a long or a short a (as in hat, hate) but as a schwa sound, a vowel almost devoid of any individual, distinctive sound. The **ou** combination of **around** is pronounced as an **ow**, being the diphthong form. In the word **night**, the i is pronounced long, and the **gh** combination is entirely silent.

It would be very easy to use the example above to state that English phonics is a hopeless mess, and that it is just as efficacious to use the "look-say" method of teaching reading rather than to get stuck in a quagmire of rules and more rules. Before responding to this statement, I wish to digress into another area: the teaching of mathematics.

No one would expect a child to do calculus immediately after learning to count. Math is recognized as a structured subject. One has to know that a certain symbol stands for a certain quantity, and the subject is begun with teaching the child to count and to use the designated number symbols: 1,2,3,4,5,6,7,8,9, and 0. Arithmetic is nothing more than manipulating quantities with only four operatives: addition, subtraction, multiplication, and division. Algebra utilizes the idea of unknowns, and introduces the concept of equations, whereby an unknown can be found if knowns are in the equation. Calculus is an advanced method for the calculation of quantities acting in complex relationships. The point of the above discussion is that phonics, too, has levels of difficulty. Words like hat, hot, bet, bit, and but are far easier to learn than words like caution, exhaust, courteous, beauty, initial, and distinguish. Lack of recognition of this point has led to the current low opinion of many educators concerning the value of phonics in reading.

In designing this book, I have acknowledged the fact that degrees of difficulty do exist in phonics by dividing this book into five levels. The first level utilizes simple phonic rules that are straightforward. The inevitable exercises (examples, really) are given, and then stories that utilize the learned phonic skills are presented. The attractive aspect of my method is the introduction of stories at different phonic levels that contain no phonic difficulties not previously explained. The child has the satisfaction of doing actual reading at an easy phonic level and quickly gains facility with words and the requirement of reading from left to right. After Level One, more phonic rules are introduced, with explanations and exercises. Then, stories that utilize these newly acquired skills are given. The same method applies to subsequent levels until Level Five, which completes the coverage of all (except the most exotic) phonic difficulties that English presents. A child finishing this book can read anything, but this does not mean that he will automatically understand everything he reads. I must emphasize that phonics is a method for pulling coded symbols off a page and converting them into sound. If a child cannot understand the subject matter when he hears it, he will not magically understand it when he reads. Phonics is a tool that enables a person to decode stored information. This is perhaps the most important skill that a teacher can impart to a student, without which a child cannot gain true independence.

CONTENTS

Introduction....................................... 1
The letters of the alphabet 11
The importance of the alphabet................. 12
How to use this book 16

READING LEVEL ONE

For the teacher 17
Long and short vowel sounds - the silent e rule 18
    The short a sound 19
    The long a sound 23
    The short i sound 24
    The long i sound 25
    The short o sound 26
    The long o sound 27
    The short u sound 28
    The long u sound 28
    The short e sound 29
    The long e sound 30
Consonants 31
Letter K special spellings 32
    The ck sound 33
Letter S special sounds 34
Digraphs 36
    The ch digraph 37
    The sh digraph 38
    The th digraph 39
    The wh digraph 40
    The ng digraph 40

Contents

Consonant clusters - introduction 41

    The st cluster 42

    The nt cluster 42

    The nd cluster 43

Consonant-vowel combinations - introduction .. 43

    The or sound 44

    The er sound 44

Miscellaneous

    Special words to and do 45

    Off vs. of 45

Summary of level one phonic rules 46

Level One stories

    The Lake 49

    The Robe 55

    The Hike 62

    Pals 67

READING LEVEL TWO

Consonant blends 72

    Initial consonant blends. 73

    Final consonant blends 74

Syllables 75

    Division between doubled consonants . . . 76

    Division between dissimilar consonants . 77

    In composite words 77

    When a consonant separates two vowels . . 78

Endings that lengthen the final vowel........ 79

    the ing ending 80

    The er ending 83

    The ed ending 84

    The le ending 86

    The y ending 88

Syllabification 89

Diphthongs 92

    The oi and oy diphthongs 93

    The ei and ey diphthongs 94

The two sounds of letter c 95

The two sounds of letter g 98

Summary of level two phonic rules 100

Level Two stories

    The Race 103

    The Camping Trip 108

    The Hut 112

    The Ship 117

Contents

READING LEVEL THREE

Long vowel sounds 122
    The long sound of letter a 122
    The long sound of letter o 123
    The double o (oo) sound 125
    The ou combination 126
    The long e sound 127
    The ie and ei combinations 128
    The long i sound 130
    The long u sound 131
The schwa 132
Letter r and the schwa 134
Unstressed endings 138
The spellings of to, too, and two 142
Miscellaneous
    Letter q 143
    Letter x 143
Summary of level three phonic rules 145
Level Three stories
    The Flute 148
    A Birthday Party 152
    The Picnic 157
    The Chess Champ 162

READING LEVEL FOUR

Diphthongs concluded...................... 167
    The ou (ow) diphthong 167
    The ew diphthong 168
The au (aw) combination 169
The hiatus 170
Silent consonants 171
    Letters b and d 172
    Letters g and h 173
    The gh combination 174
    Letters k, l, and n 175
    Letters p, s, and t 176
    Letter w 177
Silent vowels........................... 178
    Silent u 178
    Silent o 179
The ou combination, the six sounds 179
The ea combination, the three sounds 181
Digraphs concluded...................... 183
    The ph digraph 183
    The gh digraph 184
How many syllables in a word? 184
Compound words 186
Miscellaneous........................... 187
    The word <u>one</u> 187
    The y sound of i 188
Summary of level four phonic rules 189
Level Four stories
    The Locksmith 192
    The Paper Route 197
    The Show Horse 203
    The Restaurant 208

Contents

READING LEVEL FIVE

Consonant sound change before letter u 214
    The tu and du combinations 215
The ti, si, and ci combinations 216
The sh sound as in sugar 218
The zh sound as in treasure 219
The prefix 220
The suffix 221
Words used as both nouns and verbs 227
Accent and consonant doubling before a suffix. 230
Plurals 231
Miscellaneous. 236
    Deriving phonic rules 237
    Unphonic words. 240
Summary of level five phonic rules 241
Level Five stories
    The Treasure 245
    The Toy Store 254
    The Detective Agency 263
    Starting Supper 270
    The Country Club 279

THE LETTERS OF THE ALPHABET

A a   B b   C c   D d   E e   F f   G g   H h

I i   J j   K k   L l   M m   N n   O o   P p

Q q   R r   S s   T t   U u   V v   W w   X x

Y y   Z z

There are twenty-six letters in the alphabet and forty-four sounds that are made from them. Obviously, some letters have to do double and even triple duty. The student should know all the letter sounds instantly by sight. If not, more drill in letter recognition should be given before beginning this book. The above letters are in the type that is used in this book, and the student should be familiar with them before starting Level One.

THE IMPORTANCE OF THE ALPHABET

The invention of the earliest known alphabet is attributed to the Phoenicians. Their alphabet was developed about three thousand years ago in the area that is now Lebanon. The Phoenicians developed a writing system based on the idea that a symbol could stand for a specific sound. Since they were a trading people, this greatly simplified the recording of their commercial transactions. The Greeks, their trading partners, saw the advantages of a system in which written symbols could be the basis of recording speech on paper, an alternative to a picture-symbol system of writing such as the hieroglyphics of the Egyptians. The Greeks adopted the idea for an alphabet from the Phoenicians and even used many of their letters; however, they made three very important distinctions. While the Phoenicians read from right to left, as the Hebrews still do today, the Greeks developed a system in which the letters (symbols) were pronounced in succession from left to right. The second distinction was the addition of vowels to the alphabet. The Phoenician alphabet consisted of 22 characters, all consonants. The reader had to fill in the vowel sounds between the consonants, as is the case in modern Hebrew. (However, diacritical marks have been developed to aid in filling in the correct vowel, but they are often not used.) The third distinction is that all the names of the letters were not the same as the sounds of the letters. The Greeks had to adapt the alphabet to their own language which had completely different sounds from that of the Phoenician language. This change was accomplished most easily by assigning sounds to the symbols that were not the same as the names of the symbols. After much experimentation, the Greeks had an excellent system whereby every sound (phoneme) of their spoken language could be represented by a symbol which was one of the letters of their newly adopted alphabet. This was taught to children when they first began to read, and this difference between the name of a letter and its sound presented no special difficulties.

The Etruscans got the idea of an alphabet from the Greeks, and the Romans borrowed the idea from the Etruscans. The Roman alphabet has a very important difference from that of the Greeks. The Romans did not use the Greek names of the letters, but gave the names of the letters the same sound as the letters themselves. This worked well for the vowels, but the consonants had to have the vowel e added to make them pronounceable as a name. With this system, reading was simple. One just said the names of the letters that one looked at, from left to right, and the sound of the word was made.

With the Roman conquest of Europe, the Roman alphabet spread. The letters of the Roman alphabet were adopted by the conquered peoples. But now, new ways had to be employed to describe the unique sounds of the different languages since not all of these sounds existed in the Latin language. Problems arose, for example, when it was necessary to represent purely English sounds (such as the th in the word the) using the Roman alphabet. The solution employed was to combine the t and h into a new sound, th. A two-letter combination that forms a new sound is called a digraph.

With the addition of so many new sounds, some letters

acquired a name that was different from the sound of the letter. An example is the letter c. There is no sound that corresponds to the alphabet name. Letter c is always pronounced as either a k (cat) or an s (city). The same thing happens with the letter x. There is no correlation between the name and the sound of the letter. X takes either the ks sound as in mix or the gz sound as in exhaust.

More problems arose with the language as spellings were often very free and in disregard of phonic principles. This trend is the source of so many difficulties with modern spellings, since many errors of the past were fossilized into the language when people of authority such as Samuel Johnson, who published the first popular dictionary (1755), became the arbitrators of "correct usage".

In spite of all the changes in spellings, English is still 98 per cent phonic. The problem is that in order to decode the letters of our alphabet into words, one should have knowledge not only of basic phonic rules but also of the complexities that have crept into the language over the years. Some languages that use the Latin alphabet have developed such devices as accent marks, umlauts, tildes, etc. to represent sounds that did not exist in the Latin. English has added no such marks, which would be of great help to the beginning reader. The problem is constantly being enlarged by the eclectic nature of our language. Foreign words are added to English but pronounced as in the original language, maintaining their original spellings, minus the diacritical marks that aid pronunciation for the native speakers. These usually do not follow English phonic rules, and add to the ever-growing list of "unphonic" words.

The author of this book takes a purely phonic approach to reading. A phonic approach is necessary because this is the way the alphabet developed. The symbols (letters) are only a way of recording sounds. There is absolutely no merit in a whole-word approach to learning to read. A word is composed of individual letters which are the pronunciation keys. A word is historically designed to be decoded from left to right by sounding out the letters in sequence. If a child does not do this sequential decoding and looks only at the whole word, it becomes a meaningless symbol, and is not even an ideogram, the basic unit of Oriental languages. In Chinese, the idea of brightness is represented by a stylized drawing of the sun and the moon together. The reader has to get the idea that these two bright objects taken together represent the idea of brightness. The same is true of the idea for good. It is represented by a woman and child together. That such ideograms are inferior to an alphabet in expressing written ideas is certainly beyond serious argument.

In order to learn to read effectively, children must be taught phonics and <u>only</u> phonics. Many schools, in a compromise situation with parents who demand phonic instruction, are combining phonics with whole-word recognition. This method does <u>not</u> work, because if a child is taught to look at a word in any manner he chooses, such as moving his eyes from left to right and back again, he will be inclined to reversals, saying "god" when he sees the printed word "dog", and "saw" when the printed word is "was". To be successful in phonics, it is absolutely essential that the nature of the alphabet as a sound/symbol system be understood, and that no other method but decoding from left to right be employed. The invention of the alphabet is still one of the greatest achievements in human history, and its significance should not be lessened simply because of the ignorance of many educators in appreciating its history and importance.

HOW TO USE THIS BOOK

Most adults do not remember how they learned to read. Some learned to read readily, almost without effort, while others struggled and to this day still are unsure of newly-encountered words. Because the sound value given to a symbol (a letter of the alphabet) is determined by one's cultural tradition, there can be no such thing as learning to read by yourself. It is absolutely necessary to have someone demonstrate the sounds that the letters represent. To teach a child by my method, all that is needed is for the adult to pay attention to the rules and give the child an accurate sound representation of the letters and letter combinations. In the course of teaching, the adult will usually learn the rules in only one go-through. The child will probably need extra drill on certain points and maybe even a second reading of the book. It is recommended that the teacher read ahead, finishing the entire level before reading the text with the student.

The stories at the end of each level serve the dual functions of entertainment and of providing practice for the skills learned. If the student cannot read all aspects of the stories readily, the appropriate exercises should be studied again. My purpose is to create a knowledgeable teacher so that the student has a ready source of help in applying the rules to newly-encountered words when reading material other than that found in this book.

READING LEVEL ONE

An Easy Beginning: One-Syllable Words and Rules Without Exceptions.

FOR THE TEACHER

Anyone who instructs another is a teacher. In order to instruct someone, one does not need to have a certificate from any institution or from any person claiming to be an expert. All that one needs to do is impart information. This book is designed so that anyone who can read can teach anyone who cannot. Most of us have forgotten how we learned to read, and feel inadequate to the task without some help. This book supplies both the needed information about phonic rules and the structure by which they should be organized. In order that the information for the teacher be kept separate from the words intended as practice for the student, the following system is used: the teacher reads all the standard type, such as that used in this paragraph. Words designed for the student are in larger type, double struck to appear darker. For example, an exercise for the student, illustrating the long vowel, would appear:

cut-cute bit-bite hop-hope fat-fate pet-Pete

The teacher will understand the explanations of phonic rules readily and become the expert for the student, who may have to go over some points more than once. It is recommended that the teacher read the entire chapter before starting it with the student, but this is not absolutely necessary.

THE VOWELS OF THE ALPHABET

The names of the vowels are a, e, i, o, and u. It is important for the teacher to make sure that the student knows what a vowel is, and not just the names of the letters that are vowels. The word vowel comes from the same root that gives us the word voice. A vowel is a sound made by a continuous vibration of the vocal cords. There is no obstruction to the flow of air by the tongue or the teeth since the air passes directly from the vocal cords to the lips. Each vowel gets its distinctive sound due to different positions of the mouth. Please have the student place his hand on his neck over the voice box and say the vowel letters. The steady, voiced character of vowels will be experienced and appreciated, as will the different mouth positions for each vowel.

In pronouncing a consonant, the speaker restricts the passage of air in a way necessary to produce a sound that can be described as having "friction". Consonants are not sustained sounds as are vowels. This will be explained later in Level One.

Each vowel has two major sounds, long and short. One of the primary difficulties in reading is in determining the sound value to be given a vowel in a particular syllable. The general rule is that whenever two vowels occur within the same syllable, the first is long and the second silent.

Level One uses the simplest example of this rule, the "silent e" rule. Please note again the following examples:

cut–cute bit–bite hop–hope fat–fate pet–Pete

It will be important to point out to the student that the difference between the long sound and the short sound of a vowel determines the meaning of the word. Cut and cute have very different meanings.

Level One utilizes words that contain only one syllable. This is to minimize the student's difficulties. Rules governing vowel sounds in multiple syllable words will be taken up at higher levels.

THE SHORT A SOUND

When one says the letters of the alphabet, the names of the vowels are in the long vowel form. The short vowel sound, however, is more commonly encountered. Short vowel sounds are usually found in the middle of a syllable. Please remember that every syllable must contain a vowel or it is not pronounceable.

In the series: bat, hat, mat, rat, sat ... the at combination in each case has a different consonant before it. This initial consonant is added to the pronunciation and, consequently, changes the meaning of the word.

Please read the words below with the student and point out that the consonant before the at adds an additional sound to the pronunciation and the meaning of the word.

at
rat
hat

rat   hat

Words with at endings: (please read with the student)

bat fat hat mat pat rat sat vat nap

A fat rat sat on a hat.

Note that the article a is pronounced with the long
sound, while the a in the words above is pronounced with the
short vowel sound. The important thing is that the student
realize that letters stand for sounds, and that there is a
method for sounding out the letters that make up a word.
That method is to sound out each letter successively, from
left to right, and <u>not</u> look at the whole word and go back
and forth.

A bat did nap on a mat.

Practice words with the short a sound:

dad	sad	had	fad	lad	wad	map	rap	gap	lap
sap	tap	zap	nap	ham	bam	jam	ram	Pam	Sam
hag	bag	gag	lag	nag	rag	tag	wag	man	ban
Dan	fan	pan	ran	tan	van	tap	rap	lap	sap

Always have the student read from left to right. Some more short a sounds, without pattern as to the end sounds:

fat	tan	van	map	rat	nap	gas	tab	fan	pad
dad	bag	man	sad	ham	fan	had	wag	gag	lad
jam	rag	tan	Dan	Pam	Sam	gap	fad	pass	pan

Sam had ham and jam in a pan.
Sam sat on the lap of the sad man.
Dad had a map in the tan van.

In reading the practice sentences with the student, some letter combinations encountered will not have been discussed yet. The th sound of the and the nd sound of and will be introduced later in this chapter. If the student asks about these letter combinations, tell him the sound value and assure him that it will be explained later on.

An assumption is made that the student knows the letters of the alphabet on sight, and can immediately give the sound for each letter. To avoid confusion, only consonants with a single sound are used in Level One exercises. In the case of letter c, only the hard k sound is used. The only exception to this rule is in the case of the two sounds of letter s. These will be introduced later in this level because of their frequency, and because it is hard to write stories that do not use both sounds.

THE LONG A SOUND

The addition of a second vowel to a syllable lengthens the sound of the vowel that comes first. The added vowel is silent. The reason for this is in the definition of a syllable. A syllable cannot include more than one sounded vowel and still remain as one syllable. Because of this, an idea was devised for adding additional silent vowels to a syllable in order to indicate pronunciation for the first vowel. The most common example of this is the addition of the "silent e" at the end of a syllable. (In Level One, only one-syllable words are used.) Read the following words with the student so he can hear the lengthening of the vowel, and also have him practice these word combinations.

fat fate	hat hate	rat rate	fad fade
mad made	tap tape	gap gape	Dan Dane
pan pane	Sam same	cap cape	mat mate
man mane	at ate	pal pale	nap nape

Additional long a sounds:

late	pave	tame	sake	safe	name	ate	save
wave	Dave	rake	lake	gaze	gate	ape	lame
sale	take	mane	made	Jane	Kate	game	bake
haze	tape	fade	fate	wave	fake	vane	pane
make	male	late	hate	pave	tame	vase	same
lane	sale	wake	sane	tale	gale	wade	lame

These words get their long a sound from the second vowel in the word, the "silent e".

Jane did bake a cake to take to the sale.
The tame ape gave a wave to Dave.
Kate did hate to take the rake up the lane to
the gate.

THE SHORT I SOUND

The same rule applies to the letter i as does to the
letter a. Some words with short i sounds:

bib	fib	rib	bid	hid	kid	lid	rid	did	big
dig	jig	pig	rig	him	Jim	Kim	Tim	rim	dim
bin	did	pin	sin	tin	win	lip	nip	rip	sip
tip	zip	bit	fit	hit	kit	lit	sit	wit	pit

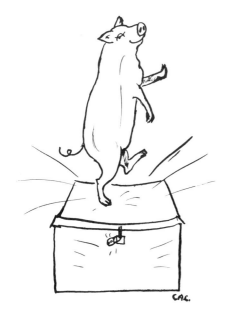

A big pig did a jig on a tin bin.

Jim had a fit and bit his lip.

The pin in the kit did not fit and made a rip in it.

THE LONG I SOUND

The "silent e" at the end of a syllable lengthens the short i to the long i sound.

hid hide	pin pine	bit bite	kit kite
sit site	Tim time	rip ripe	win wine
dim dime	bid bide	din dine	pip pipe

Some long i words:

bike	dike	pike	wide	side	hide	ride	tide
line	mine	fine	dine	pine	vine	wine	time
dime	lime	ripe	pipe	wipe	dive	hive	jive
live	site	bite	kite	mite	hike	Mike	pike
ride	tide	life	wife	rite	like	nine	vile

Tim had time to ride his bike to the dike.
   Mike had a kit to make a fine kite.
The wife did not like to sit at the site of
the big pine.

Just as in the case of letter a, the "silent e"
lengthens the preceding vowel within the same syllable.   In
Level One, only one-syllable words are used.   This is to
avoid too much complexity.   Multiple syllable words will be
taken up in Level Two.

THE SHORT O SOUND

The same rule applies to the vowel o as it did to
the vowels a and i.   Some short o sounds:

Bob	gob	lob	job	mob	sob	rob	God	hod	pod
rod	sod	Tod	nod	dog	bog	fog	hog	jog	log
tog	bop	hop	mop	pop	sop	top	dot	got	hot
jot	lot	not	pot	rot	tot	Don	Ron	mom	Tom

It had not got hot, so Bob did jog on a log.

Tod had a job to mop the top of the pot.
Tod did nod to the dog to hop on top of the sod.

THE LONG O SOUND

The addition of the "silent e" to a syllable containing an o causes the short sound to change into the long sound.

hop hope   rob robe   tot tote   rod rode   not note

Some long o sounds:

dope	hope	mope	pope	rope	dote	rote	tote
vote	bone	tone	lone	home	tome	dome	hole
mole	pole	role	sole	coke	woke	joke	poke

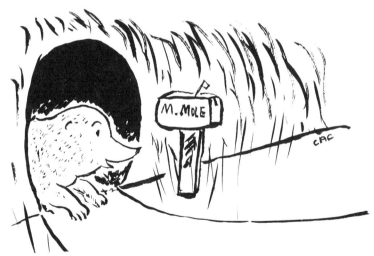

A mole has a hole for a home.
I hope to tote home the pole and rope.
I vote to put the bone in the hole as a joke on the mole.

-27-

THE SHORT U SOUND

This vowel follows the same rule as the other vowels do. Some short u sounds:

```
hub  pub  rub   tub  bud  dud  mud  sud  bug  fuss
dug  hug  jug   lug  mug  rug  tug  bum  gum  muss
hum  rum  sum   bun  fun  gun  nun  pun  run  butt
sun  but  gut   hut  nut  rut  bus  pus  putt mutt
```

The bug did lug the jug on the rug.
Cut the fuss and run to the bus.
A bug dug a rut in the mud of the hut.

THE LONG U SOUND

The u is made to get its long sound by the addition of a "silent e".

tub tube   cut cute   dud dude   mutt mute

Some long u sounds:

tune	dune	fume	nude	rude	dude	tube	lube
mule	rule	mute	lute	duke	Luke	fuse	ruse

June did use the tube in the tub.
As a rule, a mule is rude to a dude.
Luke did use the fuse as a ruse.

THE SHORT E SOUND

Some words with the short e sound:

den	hen	pen	ten	Ben	men	bet	jet	let	mess
met	net	pet	set	wet	yet	bed	led	Ned	less
red	Ted	wed	beg	peg	keg	leg	Meg	fed	Tess

The red hen set in a net in a pen.
Tess let a wet pet in the bed.
Ted led the ten men to the red keg.

THE LONG E SOUND

The e at the end of a syllable is usually long:

he   she   be   we   me

The silent e at the end of the syllable is rarely used to lengthen the sound of e, as in the word Eve. More commonly, the e is doubled to ee to get the long e sound.

```
fed feed    bet beet    ten teen    pep peep    red  reed
wed weed    Ned need    met meet    Ken keen    fell feel
```

Some practice ee words:

```
peel    feel    heel    keel    reel    feet    beet    meet
feed    seed    deed    heed    need    reed    weed    seen
teen    keen    beep    weep    deep    keep    peep    seep
```

Ned had no pep to peep at the seed on his feet.
I feel no need to feed the seed to the pet.

There are many words that have a long e sound that is made by combining another vowel with e. This combination may sound exactly like an ee combination:

week weak   peek peak   meet meat   steel steal

These vowel situations will be taken up in Level Three.

CONSONANTS

Any letter that is not a vowel is a consonant. Vowels do not restrict the flow of air from the vocal cords to the lips, whereas consonants restrict the air passage in some way. Some consonants are sounded by forcing air through a narrow passage as in the case of t, v, s, and z. Please have the student sound these consonants and note this effect.

Some consonant letters stop the sound at one point while it escapes at another: m, n, l, and r.

Some consonants produce sound by stopping and then releasing the air stream: p, t, k, b, and d.

Some consonants force air through a loosely closed passage: h, w, y, and j.

The word consonant is worth analyzing. It means to sound together. (con=with and sonant=sound). Consonants by themselves are scarcely intelligible, and need to combine with sustained sounds to carry meaning. This is why every syllable needs a vowel to be pronounceable. Consonants start and stop but do not keep the air stream flowing. That is the function of vowels. A vowel can be a syllable all by itself, but a consonant can never be.

Please repeat the previous exercises with the long and short vowels, but now pay particular attention to the pronunciation of the consonants.

It is interesting to note that some of the consonants do not utilize the vocal cords at all. The sound is made entirely by the methods listed above without vibration of the vocal cords. The five consonants that do this are: f, k, p, t, and s. These five consonants are important in certain phonic rules which will be explained and demonstrated in subsequent text.

THE LETTER K

Most consonant letters represent a single sound and present no special difficulty in reading. The letter k always represents such a single sound. Please read the following words with the student to emphasize the k sound.

kiss	keep	keel	keg	kit	kid
kite	kill	keen	Ken	Kim	kin

Ken did keep his kite in a keg.

The problem arises with the letter c. This letter has no sound of its own. It is either the sound of s or the sound of k. Please note the s sound of c:

city cigar cent cell

These words are to demonstrate a concept for the teacher. For the student, the point is to learn the k sound of letter c. Before the strong vowels a, o, and u, letter c takes the k sound. Before the weak vowels e, i, and y, letter c takes the s sound. This rule will be explained to the student in the next level. In Level One, the k sound is made with the letter k, and also with the letter c when c is before the vowels a, o, and u. Only the k sound of c is used in Level One.

Please read the following words with the student, and point out that that the letter c has the k sound.

can	cat	cap	cab	cub	cuff
cut	cup	cop	cod	cob	cot

A cat can nap on a cot.
A cop had a cut in his cap.

THE CK SOUND

Many words end in a double consonant, such as kiss, kill, egg, puff, etc. The double consonant is pronounced exactly the same as the single consonant, and it is used to ensure that the preceding vowel is pronounced short.

A common double consonant is ck. Since the letter c always has a k sound except before the vowels e, i, and y, the ck group is pronounced exactly as is the kk. If written as a formula, ck = kk. In English, kk is almost always written ck. This double consonant has the same sound as k.

Some practice words with ck:

rack	tack	sack	back	lack	hack	pock	pack
lock	rock	dock	sock	cock	hock	mock	pick
tick	kick	sick	lick	neck	hick	peck	wick
buck	luck	duck	muck	suck	tuck	deck	heck

Nick did tuck a duck in a pack on his back.
Dick did lock the sock in the sack.
The duck did peck the sick cat on the neck.

Thus, there are three ways to represent the k sound: k, c, and ck. If cat were spelled with a k, kat, it would sound the same. But there is now a very rigorous spelling system, and kat is considered to be a misspelling. That this was not always the case is evident to anyone who reads the English of the seventeenth and eighteenth centuries.

THE TWO SOUNDS OF LETTER S

Letter s has two distinctive sounds: the soft, whispered s sound that is common at the beginning of words such as six, seven, and soft, and the hard sound of s which is common at the end of words like suds, dogs, pads, and pals. The hard s sound is pronounced like a z sound.

To appreciate the reason for these two sounds of s, it is necessary to recognize the distinction between voiced and unvoiced consonants. A voiced consonant uses the vocal cords in making its distinctive sound. An unvoiced consonant does not use the vocal cords.

The unvoiced consonants are f, k, p, and t. S can be either the unvoiced hissing sound (soft) or the hard, vocal-cord z sound. The rule is: if the letter s follows an unvoiced consonant, it is unvoiced. If s follows a voiced consonant, it has the hard sound of z, its voiced counterpart. This dual pronunciation is in the interest of speech economy. If the vocal cords are vibrating when s is encountered, that s is pronounced with the vocal cords vibrating, and sounds like a z. If the vocal cords are not vibrating, as after an unvoiced consonant, it takes too much time to get the cords vibrating for the s to be sounded, and the result is the soft, unvoiced s.

Voiced and unvoiced consonants constitute a very important concept in the teaching of reading, one which will be taken up again in the higher levels. For now, please try to remember the four unvoiced consonants. A mnemonic can help: Four Kids Played Truant.

Please note the following words:

rag rags   sud suds   pad pads   pan pans   dog dogs   doll dolls

These words have the z sound of s because all of the preceding consonants are voiced.

Please read the following words with the student to demonstrate the soft sounds of s (after consonants f, k, p, and t):

nests	mats	rests	jumps	facts	rips	lips
masks	bats	pumps	huffs	sacks	sips	hips
dusts	tops	cuffs	racks	bucks	hops	tips
lumps	hats	humps	ducks	bumps	asks	cops

    The dog hops and jumps so fast that he huffs
    and puffs.
    The cat sleeps on the tops of the hats and
    makes lumps and bumps on them.

Some practice words that have the hard sound of s:

pills	runs	buns	puns	guns	beds	tubs	wigs
bills	pens	pigs	tens	dens	hens	bugs	fins
sells	pins	sins	bins	ribs	bibs	tugs	rugs
tells	figs	buns	fibs	digs	dogs	fogs	mugs
kills	hums	sums	gums	bums	puns	hogs	jogs
hills	wells	logs	wins	hugs	jugs	bells	lugs

The kids tell fibs to sell bells.
The hen kills bugs in the pens of the pigs.
The dog digs in the hills and finds bugs in logs.

Remember that the concept demonstrated by the two sounds for the consonant s is: <u>speech is usually economical in making sounds to convey information.</u> Once the vocal cords are vibrating, they usually stay vibrating when encountering another consonant. If they are not vibrating in sounding an unvoiced consonant, they don't start up again just to get the hard sound of s. This concept of sound economy is also important in understanding deemphasized vowel sounds, called schwas, which will be taken up in Level Three.

THE DIGRAPH

A digraph is a sound formed by combining two consonants to form a new sound unlike that of the letters. The word digraph means <u>two letters</u>. The two letters are used to make a sound entirely different from that of either letter alone. The mouth does not change position while sounding a digraph as it does in sounding diphthongs, the counterpart utilizing vowels, which will be discussed in a higher level.

A complete list of English digraphs:

ch	as in chief, chap, chum
gh	as in rough, tough
ph	as in phone, phonics
sh	as in she, shape, shine
th	as in the, this (hard); and in thin, thistle (soft)
wh	as in what, where, when
ng	as in sing, sang, song

All digraphs, except the ng, use the letter h. This came about because the letter h became silent in Latin, and thus was an available symbol to combine with other letters to form the new sounds.

Please note that some of the digraphs are unvoiced: ch, gh, ph, and sh. The ng is always voiced. The th and wh may or may not be voiced.

Because the ph and gh present special phonic difficulties, they will not be used in Level One but deferred until more basics have been covered.

THE CH DIGRAPH

Ch is a hissing sound that does not use the vocal cords. It is unvoiced. It is the same sound at the beginning or at the end of a word. Please read the following words with the student:

chip	chase	chum	chill	chunk	chest	chick
chop	check	chap	chess	choke	check	chime
much	punch	chat	pinch	lunch	hunch	ranch
rich	bunch	chin	bench	chimp	champ	munch

When the final ch of a word follows a vowel, a t is often inserted so that vowel is pronounced short. Some speakers pronounce this t, others do not. Both pronunciations are easily understood.

hatch	catch	match	batch	patch	notch	ditch
witch	fetch	botch	hitch	latch	itch	pitch

The witch did fetch that chest with much punch in it.
A bunch of rich chaps had lunch at the ranch.
A batch of chicks did hatch in that patch in the ditch.

THE SH DIGRAPH

The sh digraph is commonly found at both the beginning and at the end of words. It is an unvoiced sound.

shine	she	shin	shut	hash	push	sheep	shot
shell	shy	ship	bush	shop	bash	shape	dash
shame	ash	wish	hush	lash	dish	shock	rash
shore	cash	shake	mash	fish	rush	short	sash

The ship came to shore to sell fish for cash.
She did push the sash of the shop shut.

THE TH DIGRAPH

The th digraph can be hard (voiced) at the beginning of a word:

this   these   that   those   them   the   then   thus

The word <u>the</u> needs special mention. Before a following word that begins with a vowel, the final e is sounded if stressed: the apple, the egg, the ink, the oar, the usage. Before consonants, <u>the</u> is usually sounded like "thuh", where the e is unstressed and reduced to a muttering sound, called a schwa: the book, the dust, the fire, etc. This will be explained in Level Three, and is mentioned now for the teacher's information.

It is more common to encounter the soft, unvoiced th digraph, which can be at the beginning or at the end of a syllable.

three	thin	theme	thick	thug	length	thank
smith	math	cloth	broth	thud	with	worth

Those kids did thank these men for the thick broth.

This thick cloth cape with the long length is worth three of those thin, short capes.

THE WH DIGRAPH

The wh digraph is voiced. It never occurs at the end of a word.

whip   whack   whim   whiff   whisk   whale   why   what
wham   wheel   when   while   whine   white   whit whiz

The whip made a whack and a wham when it struck the white wheel.

There are words in which the wh combination is not a digraph. A digraph is a new sound that is unlike the letters used in spelling it. Before letter o the w of wh tends to be silent and in this situation the wh is not a digraph.

These are not digraph sounds of wh: who   whole   whom

Thus, for a letter combination to function as a digraph, it must produce a sound unlike that of the two spelling letters.

THE NG DIGRAPH

The ng is always voiced, and always occurs at the end of a syllable.

sing   sang   song   bang   gang   rung   hung   lung
sung   fang   hang   rang   king   ring   wing   ping

The gang did sing a song while the bells rang.

The king hung his ring on the ping-pong net.

CONSONANT CLUSTERS

Consonant clusters are letters that are frequently associated and produce distinctive sounds. These clusters resemble digraphs, but the resulting sound is not a new sound; it contains the sound of the individual letters that make up the cluster. Most of these will be taken up in Level Two. However, for the purpose of writing Level One stories, a few of the most common clusters are needed and will be introduced now. Perhaps the most common consonant cluster is the st. Please read the following list with the student:

ST Cluster:

stud	store	steep	stuck	stick	storm	step
stem	stiff	still	sting	stone	stove	stub
stop	strap	stuff	stink	staff	stack	stag

The stiff stick struck the still stone.
The hut had steep steps made of sticks and stuff.

The st is one of the few consonant clusters found at both the beginning and at the end of words:

cast	fast	last	mast	past	lust	bust	must
rust	best	rest	test	west	cost	list	mist

The best stove must cost the most and not rust like the rest.

The fast ship was lost in the mist.

Consonant clusters present no special difficulties. Two other clusters used with some frequency are the nt and the nd. These are found only at the end of words.

NT Cluster:

rent	lent	tent	dent	bent	sent	went	hint
lint	mint	tint	pant	rant	bunt	punt	runt

The man went in the tent with the bent pole.

I sent him the rent and he lent it to Kent.

ND Cluster:

band	hand	land	sand	end	bend	lend	send
tend	bond	fond	pond	and	fund	mend	wind

I am fond of the sand on the land by the pond.
Let us lend the band the funds to mend the
rents in the ends of the pants.

CONSONANT-VOWEL COMBINATIONS

There are consonants that affect the preceding and the
succeeding vowels. In Level One, only the situation of a
consonant affecting the preceding vowel is considered, and
consideration is limited to the consonant r. Letter r
affects the preceding vowels if they are short. It renders
the weaker vowels of e, i, and u into a non-descript sound
that is called a schwa, which is indicated in the dictionary
by the upside-down e symbol (ə).
Please note that before r, the e, i, and u have the
same sound:

fur   fir   her   bird   herd   curd

The stronger vowels a and o are less affected and
retain a recognizable quality of the vowel sound:

or   for   torn   port   car   far   park   farm

The above is for the teacher's information. It will be
taken up in detail in Level Three. For the purpose of
writing Level One stories, it is necessary to introduce the
er sound, which is easy to pronounce. Also, because the o
in the or combination is the least affected by the r, the or
combination is also used in Level One stories. Please read
with the student:

OR Sound:

cord	pork	porch	or	born	fort	corn
ford	lord	storm	for	fork	tore	form
cork	worn	stork	gore	sort	north	port
horn	sort	torch	torn	store	short	more

The short cord was worn and torn.
The storm tore a hole in the north porch.

ER Sound:

herd	fern	terse	Bert	nerve	jerk	verse
berg	perk	berth	term	perch	herb	serve

Bert did serve the herbs to her.
He had the nerve to perch on her berth.

MISCELLANEOUS

The purpose of the preceding material is to prepare the student for doing actual reading. Endless drill and repetition will bore most students quickly. The idea behind this book's division into reading levels is to introduce phonic rules and then present stories that utilize these rules. Level One stories contain words that have only one syllable and follow the rules given in this level. Any exception to these rules is inadvertent. If the student has difficulty with any word or words, please refer back to the pages that explain that phonic rule and then re-do the exercises.

There are words that do not follow good phonic rules. Noteable are the words to and do. It is the rule that the letter o at the end of a syllable is pronounced long. However, to is pronounced like the double o (oo) combination in the word smooth. The same thing occurs with the word do. This will have to be noted when reading with the student. The reason for this will be explained in a higher level.

The other major deviation from simple rules is the word of. The word off is pronounced according to the letter sounds. To distinguish of and off, of is pronounced as if spelled ov. The reason for this is that the voiced and unvoiced consonants have counterparts. F is the unvoiced counterpart of v. This is seen in plurals utilizing f and v, such as calf-calves, half-halves, and life-lives. When the emphasis falls on that part of a word having an unvoiced consonant, that consonant may change into the voiced counterpart, as in the f changing into a v. This will be taken up in detail in a higher level. Incidentally, z and s are voiced and unvoiced counterparts, respectively, in which case the spelling does not always change. Rules for this will be given later.

SUMMARY OF PHONIC RULES
READING LEVEL ONE

1. All syllables must contain a vowel.
2. All words in Level One contain only one syllable.
3. Vowels can be pronounced long or short. To convert a short vowel sound to the long sound, add "silent e".

> fat fate   hid hide   hop hope   tub tube   ten teen

4. Vowels have a sustained sound. Consonants have a sound in which the air stream stops and starts.
5. Letter c has two sounds. It is sounded like letter k except when followed by the vowels e, i, and the semi-vowel y. Only the k sound of c is used in Level One.

> cat   cub   cop

6. The **ck** sound is pronounced exactly the same as the k sound.
7. Letter s has two sounds, soft and hard. The soft sound follows the consonants f, k, p, and t:

> cats   masks   lips   rests

The hard sound of s, pronounced like z, follows all other consonants:

> runs beds pills ribs sums tugs

8. A digraph is a sound formed by combining two consonants into a unique sound that is unlike each of the forming letters. It is the **ch** in chap, the **sh** in she, the **th** in this (hard) or in thin (soft), the **wh** in what, and the **ng** in sing.
9. Consonant clusters are groups of consonants that are associated but retain the sound of each to a degree. Examples are the **st** of stick and fast, the **nd** of band, and the **nt** of rent.

10. The letter r affects preceding vowels. The effect is to shorten the vowel sound and make it somewhat different from the usual short-vowel sound found in words. Level One uses the or combination as in for, storm, sort, and horn. Also used in Level One is the er sound, as in her, berth, and term.

11. Usually, vowels ending a syllable are pronounced long, as in go and so. Sometimes common words violate this rule, as in to and do.

12. The word of is pronounced ov, while off has no change in the sound value of the f. This is because v is the voiced counterpart of the unvoiced f, and is used when pronunciation stress falls on the letter f.

LEVEL ONE STORIES

1. THE LAKE

2. THE ROBE

3. THE HIKE

4. PALS

Please read these stories with the student and help him with any difficulties. Then have the student read the stories to you without any assistance. If there are any problems, please note them and refer back to the appropriate pages for explanation and drill until the difficulties are mastered. Then have the student re-read the stories until all goes smoothly.

THE LAKE

Tom sat in the shade of a big bush by the side of the lake. His dog went to run on the hot sand. Tom did not chase him. The sun had made the sand hot, and Tom had bare feet. He did not feel like he had the pep to run. His dog's name was Spot. Tom got a stick and gave it a toss for Spot to chase and take back to him. Spot did like this game. When he got the stick, he bit it and went back for Tom to toss it. Spot did not seem to tire of this game.

Jan came by. She had her cat in her hands. The cat had short legs, and did not like to run in the sand. Jan sat by Tom, and put her cat in her lap. Spot came back with the stick. The cat did not like the dog, and ran to go home. The dog gave chase. The cat was not fast, as his legs sank deep in the sand. Spot did not need but a short time to catch up. Tom did not think that his dog was the type of dog that bit cats. Jan got a stone in her hand to use in case Spot did jump on her cat.

For Spot, it was the chase that was fun. When he got close to the cat, he did not go as fast. He did not want to catch the cat, but just to make the cat run fast so that it was more fun. Jan did not like it a bit that her cat had to run so fast. She got mad at Spot.

The cat ran to the shore of the lake. He did not want to get wet, nor did he want the dog to catch him. A big log was just off the shore. The cat made a big jump and got on the log. The dog came to a stop, and just sat on the sand to watch the cat. Spot did not want to keep on with the chase. It was hot.

Jan was mad at Spot for that chase of her cat. She did not want to hit him, as he was such a big dog. Tom came by to be by Spot in case Jan did use that stone she had in her fist. But Spot was a tame dog, and put his wet nose on her leg. The dog did want her to pet him. This she did,

and then put the stone back on the sand.

Jan's cat did not seem to want to jump back to the sand of the shore. The gap was a bit wide for the cat, who did not want to get wet. Tom had bare feet, and did not care if he got them wet. It was just five steps from the shore to the log. He went to the log and got the cat. As he went back with the cat, his heel hit a big thing that was stuck in the mud. It was so big that his feet did not feel the end of it. He gave the cat to Jan, and went back to see what it was. It was a big chest.

The kids ran home to tell mom and dad. Jan's dad and Tom's dad came to see what it was that was stuck in the mud. The men dug, and got the chest to the shore. The lock had so much rust on it that it just fell off. Then the kids got to help the men lift the lid and see what was in the chest.

It was full of pots and pans and things like that. The chest was in the mud for a long time, as the pans had a lot of rust on them. On the side of the chest was the name of the ship that had sunk in the lake in a bad storm when Tom's dad was just a small kid. That was a long time in the past. A kid can keep such things that he gets like this. It seems that men do not care who keeps a thing that had been lost for a long time.

Jan and Tom did share what was in the chest. It was a lot of stuff. The man at the store gave them cash for most of it, and the kids gave the rest of the stuff to mom and dad. So, the shore of the lake is not just a spot to go and run with a cat or a dog. It can be a spot to get things. When Tom gets big, he plans to get the things that he needs so that he can then seek more stuff deep in the mud of the lake.

THE ROBE

The king is the boss of all the men in the land. Pete is the son of the king. When Pete gets big, he will be the king. But that will not be for a long time, as Pete is just ten. The king lets Pete be the boss of all the kids in the land.

Pete made a rule that all kids must be at his home six times a week. He has a big home. Then Pete picks the kids to be with him, and lets the rest go home. Pete makes up the rules of all the games so that he can win all the time. Pete is the boss all the time, which makes the kids mad.

Most kids must go to bed by nine. Not Pete. He can go to bed as late as he wants to. But all kids need lots of sleep, and Pete makes up for this lack of sleep with naps. When Pete wants to take a nap, he stops the games. He makes all the kids just sit or stand by his bed while he sleeps.

Sam did not like to just sit on the rug while Pete was in bed. He put on Pete's red robe. He made up a game in which he was the boss. It was fun. Then he gave the robe to Dan. Dan did the same thing just for a short time. It was a game that kids like, a game in which no kid was the boss all the time.

But Dan was not as tall as Pete or Sam. The robe was so long that his feet got on the hem and made a mess of mud on the robe. It is Pete's rule

that no kid can put on his robe. Just he and the king had long red robes, and just he and the king put them on. Pete will wake up and see the mud on the robe, and get mad. The kids had to think fast.

Sam put the robe on the bed with Pete. Then he got Pete's dog. He put the dog's feet in the mud. Then he put the dog on top of the robe. More mud got on the robe. It was just in the nick of time. Pete woke up.

Pete did not like the mud on his robe. He got mad at the dog. Pete did not want a dog at his home that got mud on his robe. He gave the dog to Sam to take with him when he went home.

Pete then got a white cat to be his pet. Sam and Dan did the same thing with the cat. When Pete went to bed to take his nap, the kids put mud on the cat's feet. Then the cat was put on Pete's robe. This made Pete mad when he woke up, so he gave the cat to Dan.

Pete then went to the king's den and got both a cat and a dog. But the kids did the same thing. Sam put mud on the feet of the cat, and Dan put mud on the feet of the dog. The kids then put both pets on the robe. Pete got mad at those pets, and gave them to the kids. In a week's time the king had no more pets.

The king had those pets so that no rats came in to his den. But then, rats did get in the king's den. This made the king mad. Who had his pets? The kids had the pets. The king had to send a man to the pet store to get more dogs and cats. Cats and dogs will chase rats. The king made a rule that Pete had to let the cats and dogs in the den.

So, when Pete got up from his nap, the robe had no more mud on it. But the kids had no more fun, and did not like to be with Pete. The games that Pete did with the kids made them sad. It was no fun when Pete was the boss all the time.

The king got the kids' dads to see him in his den. The king did not like to see sad kids. Why was this? The dads of the kids did tell the king why. It was that Pete was the boss all the time in all the games. No kid likes that.

The king went to Pete to tell him why the kids did not like to be with him. Pete did want to do fun things with the kids. So he gave his red robe back to the king. He did not want it while he was still a kid. When he gets big, he will take it back and be the boss of men. But kids do not like a boss, and will not be a pal to a boss.

In a short time, the kids had fun with Pete. The games were fun. Pete did not need a rule to make the kids want to be with him. Pete went to bed by nine and did not take naps when the kids came to be with him. No kid was sad when he was with Pete and all had the best time.

THE HIKE

Ted and Dot went on a hike. It was the same type of hike that the gang was on last week. But at that time a storm came up and all the kids had to run home or get all wet. Ted had lost his hat, and Dot had lost her lunch box. The kids went up the same path to see if those lost things were still by the side of the path.

Ted's hat was big and red. Ted did hope that it was not hid by a tree or a rock. It did not take them long to spot it. It was by a big bush. Ted went to pick it up, but a rat came and sat on top of the hat. The rat had made the hat his home for the past week, and did not want Ted to take it. Ted did not want to get bit by that rat, and so he went back to the path with Dot.

Her lunch box was close to Ted's hat. It was green, with black and white stripes on the sides. The lid was not shut. She gave it a poke with a stick to see if a rat or a bug had made a home in it. It was not a rat or a bug but a snake that was in the box. The snake made a hiss. She ran back to the path to be with Ted. She got the creeps the time she had seen a snake in her home when she was small, and it was the same thing this time. It was just a small snake, but she did not want to run the risk of a snake bite.

Ted did not like snakes, but he did not get the creeps from them like Dot did. Still, he did want to do the safe thing. He did not want to risk a bite from that snake or that rat. The kids went home and got Ted's dog. His name was Pal, and he was big and fast. The dog did like to go with them. The kids went back up the path. Ted got a stick and went to his hat, and the dog came with him. The rat had hid in the dome of the hat. Ted gave the hat a poke and the rat went on the top of the hat. The dog ran to the hat. The rat did not like the dog and ran up the path. Pal gave chase. Ted got his hat. It was full of dust and mud, but it did not seem to be in bad shape.

He did not see cuts or rips in it. All he had to
do was shake it to get the dust and mud off. Then
he put it on. It fit him just fine.

The rat ran in a hole that was by the side of
the path. The dog was big, and did not fit in
that hole. Ted did not want his dog to get bit by
that rat, and did not like to see him dig at such
a fast rate. He did not want to let Pal go on
with that dig and made him stop. Then Ted went
with Pal to meet Dot by her lunch box. He had got
his hat back, which was why he came back to the
path this week.

Dot gave Ted a long stick. The kids went to
the lunch box. He gave the lunch box a poke with

the stick.   The snake made a hiss.   Dot ran back to the path.   The dog did want to chase and bite the snake.   The snake did not seem to want to go and hide in a hole like the rat had. This box was his home for the last week, and he did like it, and did want to keep it.

Ted gave the box a poke with the stick to get the tip stuck in the strap on the lid. He then gave the stick a pull, a bit at a time, and got the box to the path, inch by inch.   The snake did not see that Ted had the box.   The box was O.K., and Ted gave it to Dot.   Ted did not want the snake to get mad and bite his dog.   He made a wave with his hand for his dog to go on home with them. This the dog did, and let the snake sit by the path to just hiss at them.

The kids did not like snakes and rats. That path was the best spot for a hike and the kids did not want to keep off of it.   So a plan was made up.   Pal was to go with them.   A dog is brave, and will keep the rats and snakes off the path.   This made that lane a safe spot for Ted and Dot to use just as long as Pal was with them.

PALS

Ken had no pals. He was a pest, and did things to the kids on his street that no kid likes. In just a week's time he did these bad things:

Ken gave Sam's dog a bone to make him sit still. Then he put a lot of red stuff on the dog. It made the dog a deep shade of red. Sam and his dog did not like the red stuff and it did not wash off. Sam was mad at Ken.

Ken had put a bug on Dot's leg. The bug bit her, and made her leg sore. Her mom had to keep a patch on it for a week. Dot's mom did not want her to go by Ken's home. When Dot had to use that path, she ran by Ken's home so fast that he did not see her. Dot was not Ken's pal.

Ken did like to hide in the bush by his home and watch the kids go by. Dan came up the path. Dan did not see the mud pond that Ken had made by the path with his hose. Ken went in back of Dan and gave him a push. Dan fell in the mud. Then Ken got the hose and made Dan all wet. This made Dan so mad that he went to grab the hose and do the same thing back to Ken. But Ken had run in his home and was safe. Ken's mom was not at home, so Dan did not tell her what Ken did to him this time. Dan was not Ken's pal, not at all.

Mike had a big hat that he wore all the time. It was white, with a red band. Mike went by Ken's home a lot, as his home was just up the lane. Ken got a long pole and put a pin on the tip of it. Then he hid in the bush with his pole. When Mike went by, Ken gave the hat a poke with the pole to bump it off so that it fell on the path. Then he stuck the hat with the pin. All he had to do was pull the pole back in the bush, and he had Mike's hat in his hand. This made Mike mad. He gave chase, but Ken had run so fast and hid so well in back of a big tree that Mike did not see him. But Mike was in luck. Dot, Dan, and Sam had been on a bike ride, and came up the path just then. Mike gave a wave for them to come to him. Mike had a lot of pals. Ken did not want all those kids to gang up on him, so he ran for his home. But a kid can not run as fast as a kid can go on a bike. Dan and Sam went up the lane so fast and cut off that path home for Ken. Ken did not keep on the same path, but went by a short cut to his home. He had put Mike's hat on a tree branch, so Mike did get his hat back. But Mike was still mad at Ken.

Just then Ken's mom came up the lane. She had a bag full of things from the store. The kids were mad, and went to tell her all the bad things Ken did this past week. It made her sad. She had cake and gum in her bag. She gave it to the kids. She got it for Ken, but as long as he is such a bad kid he will get no more.

The gang of kids made a rule that no kid was to go by Ken's home. Ken had no pals at all and

no cake or gum. This was no fun. The gang went on bike rides, but not with him. The gang went on hikes, but not with Ken.

Ken's dad was not mad at him. He did not like the tricks that Ken did to the kids, but still gave him a dime when he put the trash in the trash can. Ken went to the store to get a pack of gum. The gang from his street was at the store. Just then a bunch of big kids came by and put a hive of bees in the store for a joke. Ken did not think that it was fun to get stung. He got a can from the shelf that had stuff in it to chase bugs. The bees did not like the smell of the mist that came from the can and went to the vents to get back to the trees and grass. The gang was glad that Ken came in the store when he did. No kid likes to get a bee sting. Ken did tell the kids that he did not want to do bad things like those big kids who put that hive in the store. He did want to have pals. Ken gave all the kids in the gang a share of his gum. He had not made them mad at him this past week. He had made the bees go from the store. So, the kids on his street let him try to be a pal. The kids let him go with them on a hike and on a bike ride. It was not long 'till Ken was in the gang on his street. This was the most fun of all. No more bad deeds for Ken!

READING LEVEL TWO

Two-Syllable Words and Letter Combinations
That Build More Complex Words.

CONSONANT BLENDS

Consonant blends are successive consonant sounds within a syllable. For example, in the series **rap, trap, strap,** additional consonants do not change the sounds of the consonants to which they are added. Each consonant is clearly heard when the word is properly pronounced. Thus, consonant blends present no special difficulty to the student. It is necessary to point out the additive aspect of successive letters, and that is all. This helps in spelling, since properly pronounced consonant blends are written just as they are pronounced.

Please remind the student of the difference between a consonant blend and a digraph. A digraph, unlike a consonant blend, is made from a combination of consonants that <u>cannot</u> be pronounced in succession. It is a way of using two letters together in order to create a new sound not expressible with only a single letter. This concept becomes very important in the more advanced levels of phonic instruction. Digraph vowel-consonant combinations cannot be properly pronounced by simply sounding out the letters in a successive manner because digraphs represent new sounds that are unlike the sounds of the names of the letters that make them up. The confusion arises when the student insists that the <u>names</u> of the letters are the same as the <u>sounds</u> of the letters. This is generally true, but it is not true in the case of digraphs and other vowel-consonant combinations that will be explained in higher levels.

Below is a list of the most common consonant blends. Please read this with the student, pointing out the additive nature of these consonant combinations. The word changes meaning with the addition of subsequent letters, of course.

Initial Consonant Blends

bl	lack black	lend blend	lock block	less bless
br	rat brat	ring bring	rag brag	rave brave
cl	lip clip	lamp clamp	lap clap	lump clump
cr	rust crust	rest crest	rash crash	rate crate
dr	rug drug	rip drip	rag drag	rank drank
fl	lock flock	lash flash	lag flag	lake flake
fr	rock frock	rank Frank	red Fred	risk frisk
gl	lint glint	lobe globe	loss gloss	land gland
gr	rip grip	race grace	rim grim	raze graze
pl	lace place	lot plot	lug plug	lane plane
pr	rank prank	rim prim	robe probe	ride pride
sc	cat scat	cab scab	can scan	care scare
scr	roll scroll	rap scrap	ram scram	rub scrub
str	rap strap	ride stride	ring string	rip strip
sk	kid skid	kin skin	kit skit	kill skill
sl	lip slip	lap slap	lot slot	lack slack

sm	mall small	mile smile	mug smug	mash smash
sn	nap snap	nip snip	nob snob	nag snag
sp	pit spit	pill spill	pot spot	pace space
st	top stop	tick stick	tall stall	tore store
sw	well swell	weep sweep	wing swing	wore swore
tr	rust trust	rap trap	rip trip	rash trash
tw	wine twine	win twin	wig twig	weed tweed

Some Final Consonant Blends

ct	act	fact	tact	duct	pact		
ft	left	lift	raft	gift	soft		
ld	held	meld	gild	weld			
lf	elf	self	golf	gulf			
lk	milk	silk	sulk	bulk			
lm	elm	film	helm	calm			
lp	help	gulp	pulp	yelp			
lt	belt	felt	melt	pelt	hilt	jilt	silt
mp	camp	bump	jump	limp	pump	ramp	lump
nd	and	band	hand	end	tend	mend	fund
nk	bank	sink	ink	sank	sunk	wink	bunk
nt	tent	bent	hint	dent	sent	tint	rent
pt	apt	kept	wept	rapt			
sk	ask	risk	desk	task	mask	dusk	tusk
sp	asp	lisp	gasp	rasp			
st	must	fast	west	rust	nest	pest	vast

It is not necessary that the student understand the meaning of the above words. What is important is that he recognizes the concept of additive consonant sounds. It is very important that he proceeds from left to right, sounding out as he goes. He should never move his eyes back and forth over the letters, as this leads to reversals and confusion. All reading systems using an alphabet are designed to be sounded out as a progression of sounds. In phonics there is no such thing as whole-word recognition. It is a letter recognition process as the eyes pass from left to right over the word.

SYLLABLES

Up to now, only one-syllable words have been used to demonstrate phonic rules. This was done to avoid introducing too many rules at one time. It is worth noting that phonic rules apply to individual syllables, and not necessarily to the word as a whole. If a complex word is broken down into its individual syllables, the phonic rules are applied to each syllable as a unit, and then the syllables are sounded in succession. One of the most important aspects of reading is the proper division of a word into its syllables. This is the main subject of Reading Level Two.

A syllable is a word, or part of a larger word, that is pronounced with a single, uninterrupted sounding of the voice. A vowel may make up an entire syllable. A consonant by itself never makes up a syllable. The word syllable means that which holds together. A syllable is a unit, and it is independent of the other syllables in the word except for stress emphasis.

In introducing the student to syllable division, it is easiest to start with the most consistent situation. This is division between doubled consonants. Please read the list below with the student. In each word, syllable division occurs between doubled consonants. Please note that the double consonant is pronounced exactly the same as a single consonant, and the sound of the consonant goes with the preceding syllable. The purpose of the double consonant is not to pronounce the consonant twice, but to keep the vowel short in the preceding syllable. Please remember that a syllable must have a vowel in order to be pronounced.

Syllable Division Between Doubled Consonants

rabbit	better	hello	fatter	latter
happen	bigger	comma	biggest	zipper
bitter	buzzer	holly	spotted	winner
supper	puzzle	puppy	trapper	attack
sadder	sizzle	apple	chatter	differ
sudden	assist	fussy	command	attend
common	nugget	fiddle	comment	ribbon
tunnel	riddle	dinner	shutter	nozzle
fibber	rudder	butter	slipper	wetter

In the initial pronunciation of these words there will be a slow emphasis on each syllable, and the second syllable will tend to begin with the consonant sound. Thus, the double consonant will tend to be heard twice: at the end of the first syllable and at the beginning of the second syllable. This is acceptable for the student. However, at some point the student should be encouraged to say the entire word with some speed, and the two consonant sounds of the double consonant will merge automatically into one which will go with the preceding syllable.

Syllable Division Between Consonants

In words in which the vowels are separated by two consonants that are not the same (doubled), the syllable split occurs between these consonants. Again, please remember that each syllable must have a vowel. When reading longer words that have more than one syllable, the eyes pass from left to right. Because a syllable can have but one and only one vowel, the student is alerted that the end of the syllable is near as soon as he encounters the vowel. He looks for the doubled consonant or two consonants in a row that do not constitute a digraph or a consonant blend. Please read the following list with the student keeping the above comments in mind.

napkin	nap kin		dentist	den tist
basket	bas ket		blister	blis ter
winter	goblin	compose	upset	formal
number	sandal	combine	under	sunset
campus	canvas	confess	orbit	wonder
doctor	picnic	welfare	order	corner
cactus	walrus	thunder	unfit	inform
border	content	witness	monster	former

Syllable Division In Composite Words

Please note that in composite words the split occurs between the words that make up the larger word. Also, please note that splits do not occur between digraphs and consonant blends.

bathtub	bath tub	dishpan	dish pan
tinsmith	tin smith	dustpan	dust pan

lipstick	upset	locknut	tinsmith	bulldog
baseball	lapdog	postman	locksmith	hatrack
softball	hotrod	caveman	landscape	milkman
bathrobe	tomcat	lifelong	checkmate	bagpipe
grandson	sunset	chopstick	springtime	hilltop
landlord	bullpen	hitchhike	gravestone	lineman

A Single Consonant Separating Two Vowels

Whenever there is a single consonant that separates two vowels, the syllable split usually gives the consonant to the following syllable. A vowel at the end of a syllable is usually pronounced long. Please read the following with the student:

silent	si lent	label	la bel	motor	mo tor
		soda	so da		

stupid	unite	began	virus	odor	focus
flavor	minor	minus	total	unit	rival
locate	rifle	cider	polar	donate	pilot
tomato	cedar	label	labor	potato	bonus

(Tomato and potato are three-syllable words, but are included here because they illustrate the point so well.)

Please note that the double consonant between syllables is very important in determining the pronunciation of the vowel (long or short) in the first syllable. The following examples should be read with the student, pointing out the difference in sound and meaning that occurs when there is only one vs. two consonants (doubled) separating syllables:

hoping	hopping
diner	dinner
coma	comma
holy	holly
ruder	rudder
fiber	fibber
filing	filling
planed	planned
super	supper
taping	tapping
liking	licking
scraping	scrapping

In the first column, the consonant goes with the second syllable, and the vowel is pronounced long. In the second column, the consonant sound goes with the first syllable, and the vowel is pronounced short. The change in meaning accompanying the change from the short to the long vowel sound is obvious.

ENDINGS THAT LENGTHEN THE VOWEL: THE 'SILENT E' EFFECT

In Level One the emphasis was on the short and long forms of the vowel. The only way shown to lengthen a vowel was the addition of a 'silent e' at the end of the word. There are word endings that do the same thing. The addition of the endings ing, ed, er, le, and y will cause the preceding vowel to lengthen. Please note this effect as demonstrated in the following words:

like	liked	liking	
name	named	naming	
rave	raved	raving	
hope	hoped	hoping	
wipe	wiped	wiping	wiper
rule	ruled	ruling	ruler

If, when one of the endings ing, ed, er, le, and y is added to a word, it is necessary to keep the preceding vowel short, then the consonant before these endings must be doubled. Please review the list on the previous page with the student and keep this concept in mind. It is one of the most useful rules in spelling.

The doubled consonant determines that the syllable break falls between its two letters, and also determines that the vowel in the preceding syllable will be short. Without the doubled consonant, the first syllable ends with a vowel, pronounced long, and the consonant is pronounced with the second syllable. Specific practice with this concept follows.

The ING Ending

In Level One, it was shown that a 'silent e' at the end of a word causes the preceding vowel to be pronounced long, provided that there is only one consonant between the silent e and the vowel. Hop becomes hope. The same is true for the ing ending. Please note with the student:

hope	hoping	like	liking	file	filing
gaze	gazing	name	naming	dine	dining
rave	raving	wipe	wiping	rule	ruling

If, however, when an ing ending is added to a word and the preceding vowel is to be kept short, then it is necessary to double the final consonant before the ing. Please note:

hop	hopping	sob	sobbing	spin	spinning
dip	dipping	mop	mopping	whip	whipping

The reason for this lies in syllable division. A syllable is a unit. The double consonant is the place where the word is divided into separate syllables (units). Syllables do not affect each other as far as basic pronunciation is concerned.

Please read the following list with the student, noting the syllable split between the doubled consonants and the short vowel of the first syllable. When the word is spoken slowly, with a slight pause between the syllables, both of the doubled consonants tend to be pronounced. The consonant is heard at the end of the first syllable and again at the beginning of the second. With more rapid pronunciation and a shorter interval between the syllables, only one sound for the doubled consonant is heard, occuring at the end of the preceding syllable.

grabbing	buzzing	stunning	spinning	tugging
whipping	padding	dragging	shopping	canning
stabbing	fibbing	skipping	brimming	nagging
stirring	sitting	flipping	rubbing	setting
skimming	begging	slipping	dipping	betting
drumming	sagging	sledding	tipping	bedding
trimming	fitting	shipping	sobbing	budding

Some practice words with a long vowel sound in the first syllable:

liking	filing	lining	rating	gazing
fading	hoping	dining	grating	raving
wiping	taping	naming	hating	dating

Some practice words that have an ing ending after two consonants. Note that no doubling of the final consonant is needed to keep the final vowel short:

walking	lifting	talking	jumping	planting
pulling	brushing	singing	bumping	climbing
rocking	licking	dumping	pushing	swinging

Some practice words in which the vowel is long. No doubling of the consonant is used in the spelling, as that will not affect the vowel sound.

sleeping	bleeding	meeting	greeting	seeding
weeding				

In the last two example categories above, please note that the syllable break is such that the ing forms its own syllable:

walking   walk ing   sleeping   sleep ing

It is a general rule that suffixes (and prefixes) form separate syllables when attached to words. The exception is the case when the ing substitutes for the final e (the silent e) in a word.

The concept that the teacher should explain to the student is this: A vowel at the end of a syllable is usually pronounced long. A doubling of the consonant occurs when that vowel is to be pronounced short; then, the syllable does not end in a vowel. The student already knows that different meanings are transmitted by the difference in a long and a short vowel. Please remind the student that hop and hope are very different words, and so are hoping and hopping. The difference is in the syllable break.

hoping has the long o sound

hopping has the short o sound

This same concept applies to the following headings, which are the other endings that have an effect similar to the ing ending. These endings are er, ed, le, and y.

The ER Ending

The same rule concerning the ing ending applies to the er ending. To keep the preceding vowel short, it is necessary to double the final consonant before the er ending. Note that the syllable division occurs between the doubled consonants.

better	shopper	upper	letter	dipper
ladder	slipper	dinner	fatter	winner
bigger	drummer	summer	chatter	robber
patter	dresser	pepper	skipper	hammer
supper	stopper	rubber	glimmer	banner

If there is more than one consonant before the er ending, then no doubling of the final consonant occurs.

helper	snicker	locker	farmer	jumper
rocker	flicker	tumbler	golfer	pester

Please note that an er ending added to a word in which the last two letters are consonants is pronounced as a separate syllable.

farm er   help er   jump er   rock er

If the vowel is to be kept long, then no doubling of the final consonant is necessary before the er ending:

ruler	maker	baker	driver	fiber	diner
hiker	diver	super	clover	Dover	miner

Here, the consonant goes with the er suffix:

ru ler   ma ker   ba ker

The above is an example of the general rule that whenever one consonant separates two vowels, that consonant usually goes with the second syllable, and a vowel at the end of a syllable is pronounced long.

The ED Ending

The ed ending has the same effect as the ing and the er endings. It causes the final vowel of the word to be lengthened if separated by a single consonant, the same effect as the 'silent e'. Please read with the student:

file filed	wipe wiped	rage raged	pipe piped
bake baked	tape taped	hire hired	time timed
size sized	fire fired	fake faked	page paged

In words in which the short vowel is to be preserved, the consonant before the ed is doubled:

batted	matted	pitted	fitted	patted
potted	petted	budded	kidded	wetted
nodded	padded	betted	spotted	wedded

In the list just above, all the words are examples of the doubling of a t or a d before the ed ending. Note that in the words in this list the ed is a separate syllable. Although the syllable break comes between the doubled syllable, the second letter (the consonant before the ed) is not sounded.

By contrast, note again the first list under this heading. In words like filed, raged, and wiped, the ed does not form a separate syllable, but tacks on to the end of the word. Indeed, in these sample words, the ed is reduced to only a d or a t sound.

The rule concerning whether or not the ed is tacked on or pronounced as a separate syllable is simple. After a d or a t, the ed is a separate syllable. After all other letters, it is tacked on and not pronounced as a separate syllable. The reason for this is found in the nature of how the letters d and t are formed. They are voiced and unvoiced counterparts. The d is the voiced counterpart of the unvoiced t. Both are sounded by stopping the air flow and then suddenly releasing it. When the air is stopped and released to form a d or a t, nothing can be added, as that sound is spent. The ed has to be a separate syllable to be sounded.

Read the following list with the student, and note that the ed ending is not pronounced as a separate syllable, but just added on. This occurs automatically.

robbed	stopped	nagged	bossed	hissed
fussed	skipped	bucked	miffed	buzzed
tipped	snapped	puffed	kicked	pinned
rolled	dropped	fussed	huffed	canned
kissed	blessed	picked	planned	bagged
jerked	clogged	socked	blessed	rocked
jumped	crammed	locked	trapped	bumped
mocked	stuffed	ducked	slammed	packed
ticked	flipped	missed	shrugged	lacked
massed	whipped	tossed	repelled	mussed

The teacher will notice a subtle difference in pronouncing the final d of the ed ending. Sometimes it is a d and other times a t. Please remember the unvoiced consonants that were listed in Level One. They are f, k, p, t, and s. Whenever the final d follows an unvoiced consonant, it has the unvoiced equivalent sound of t. Please re-read the above list with this in mind, and it becomes evident. This is a subtle effect, and occurs automatically. It is noted for the teacher's information, and may or may not be explained to the student at this time.

The LE Ending

The le ending also participates in the doubling of the final consonant to keep the last vowel short. Please read with the student:

hobble	riddle	bottle	apple	coddle
meddle	muddle	fizzle	little	bubble
puzzle	guzzle	cuddle	snuggle	cattle
bubble	settle	sizzle	brittle	fiddle
nipple	muzzle	saddle	prattle	paddle
dazzle	peddle	babble	cripple	raffle
rattle	battle	tattle	drizzle	kettle

The le ending does not cause the final consonant before it to be doubled if that consonant is the second of two consonants. This is the same rule encountered already with the ing, er, ed, and now the le ending.

humble	mangle	jingle	ample	candle
fumble	pickle	tangle	angle	handle
single	jangle	simple	uncle	tackle
sample	dimple	temple	stumble	pimple
mumble	rumble	humble	crackle	nimble
handle	jungle	fickle	grumble	bustle
dangle	hustle	sickle	thimble	rustle

Here are some le words in which the vowel is long:

cradle	bible	able	idle	ladle
staple	bugle	gable	maple	cable
bridle	Mable	table	stable	fable

Some spelling hints: if one is in doubt in spelling a word as to whether or not the final consonant before the endings ing, er, le, and ed is a single or a double consonant, one need only pronounce the word. A short vowel indicates a double consonant, and a long vowel a single consonant.

The Final Y

The final y of a word has the same effect upon the last vowel of a word as do the endings ing, er, ed, and le. But this happens only when the word means "having the qualities of" and not when the y is part of the adverb ending ly. The consonant before the y must be double to prevent the preceding vowel from becoming long.

Please read with the student:

mud	muddy	sun	sunny	fun	funny	dad	daddy
fog	foggy	wit	witty	pup	puppy	Ted	Teddy
bag	baggy	sag	saggy	Peg	Peggy	mom	mommy
Tom	Tommy	pen	penny	nut	nutty	Tim	Timmy
cat	catty	sis	sissy	fat	fatty	rat	ratty

kitty	bunny	dizzy	penny	hilly	fussy
mommy	runny	caddy	paddy	fuzzy	giddy
muggy	lobby	Billy	silly	chilly	Sally
bully	taffy	jiffy	puffy	snappy	Jeffy
happy	poppy	messy	dizzy	stuffy	Danny

In the above list, the y is pronounced as a long e sound. This applies when the words are pronounced separately, as when reading a list. However, when such words are used in continuous speech, the y takes on the qualities of a short i terminal sound, a sound that indicates nothing is to follow in the word, and that the word is finished.

Daddy gave the fussy kitty to mommy.
The funny bunny had a runny nose.
It was sunny and muddy at the same time.

Some examples of a long vowel sound when there is only one consonant separating the final y:

hazy baby crazy lazy

The letter y is the only letter that can behave as both a consonant and a vowel. Y is a consonant only when it begins the word or syllable, and functions as a vowel elsewhere in the syllable. Some words in which y is a consonant:

yes   yet   yuck   yak   yank   yard
yell   yoke   yule   yarn   yap   yum-yum

At the end of a short word, the y is pronounced as a long i:

sky   my   by   **shy**   fly   dry   cry   **why**   try

This is because the word has no other vowel, and the long i sound makes the word more easily intelligible.

SYLLABIFICATION

The concept behind syllabification is to split a word of more than one syllable into pronounceable parts. This is primarily to indicate the proper vowel sounds, long or short. More complicated rules will be introduced later. The general rules introduced in Level Two are:

Syllable breaks occur between double consonants:

rabbit	rab bit	dinner	din ner	happen	hap pen
puppy	pup py	riddle	rid dle	summer	sum mer

Splits into syllables generally occur between consonants, provided the consonants are not digraphs or consonant blends:

napkin	nap kin	hamster	ham ster
kitchen	kit chen	lobster	lob ster
dangling	dang ling	butcher	but cher

If there is only one consonant between vowels, the consonant usually goes with the following syllable, and the vowel that ends the first syllable is usually pronounced long:

flavor	fla vor	locate	lo cate	cider	ci der
cedar	ce dar	donate	do nate	tulip	tu lip

It would be nice indeed if this were all there was to division into syllables. There is a major exception to the last rule above. If there is only one consonant between two vowels, and the first vowel is to be pronounced short, then the consonant goes with the first syllable in determining the syllable break.

Please read the following list with the student:

linen	lin en	solid	sol id	modern	mod ern
rapid	rap id	river	riv er	tropic	trop ic
limit	lim it	panel	pan el	credit	cred it
visit	vis it	lemon	lem on	second	sec ond
model	mod el	modest	mod est	chapel	chap el
level	lev el	travel	trav el	shovel	shov el

It would be ideal if all of the above words had double consonants at the syllable break. Then the first syllable vowel would be pronounced short without any doubt. This brings up a fundamental aspect of reading. Reading is decoding, converting symbols (letters) into sound. If the reader doesn't understand the word in his speaking vocabulary, he will not understand it in his reading vocabulary, as they are the same vocabulary.

In the above list, the reader has to already know the word to determine where the syllable break is. By this, I mean that in the word <u>linen</u> the reader has to already know that the first vowel is short, and then put the consonant <u>n</u> at the end of the first syllable. This is easy for the experienced reader, but for the beginner it presents a difficulty that can be resolved in only one way: trial and error. If, in first encountering the word linen, the reader breaks it down into li nen, with the i long, the resultant word makes no sense. The reader then has to try it the alternate way, lin en. With a short i, and the first syllable lin, the sound makes up the understandable word linen. I wish to point out that this is <u>not</u> word guessing. Guessing has no real direction behind it, but trial and error does. In the above example, there are only two choices. In any reading situation, a knowledge of phonic rules narrows the possibilities to only a few, which speeds up the reading process and enhances accuracy.

DIPHTHONGS

A diphthong is a vowel sound that results from a combination of two vowel sounds to form a new sound. It is a complex sound in which there is a glide from one sound to another in the course of pronouncing the diphthong. The word diphthong means "two utterances". It is the vowel counterpart to the digraph which is a sound represented by two consonants.

In Level One, it was noted that there are only seven digraphs. Diphthongs are even simpler. There are only four: oi (oy), ei (ey), ou (ow), and ew. A complete list:

OI and OY. In the vowel combinations oi as in boil and oy as in boy, the same sound is made. The only difference is in their spellings. The oi spelling usually occurs inside a word and the oy spelling at the end of a word. Please note that the y functions as a vowel.

> coin   point   boy   toy

EI as in neighbor and weigh

EY as in they

These spellings, ei and ey, are alternate spellings of the same sound.

OU as in about

OW as in cow

These are different spellings for the same sound. The ou is usually found within the word and the ow is found at the end of the word.

EW as in few, new, chew.

A diphthong is by definition made up of two vowel sounds. There is a slight change in mouth position while pronouncing the diphthong, with a glide from one part of the sound to the other. Please note that a diphthong counts for only one vowel when determining syllable breaks and pronunciation. There cannot be two separate vowel sounds in any one syllable. A diphthong comes close to doing that, but not quite. So, when encountering the vowel combinations noted above, the reader is alerted to the possibility of a diphthong because of the impossibility of pronouncing each of the vowels within the same syllable.

It has already been noted that the letter y functions as a vowel in all cases except at the beginning of a word or syllable. The letter w can take on the qualities of a vowel, as it does in the ow diphthong (e.g. cow) and the ew diphthong (e.g. few). This is not surprising, as w is really double u.

In Level Two, only the oi (oy) and the ei (ey) diphthongs will be introduced to the student. The above is for the teacher's information, and will be explained to the student later.

The OI and OY Diphthongs

There is no way to learn to pronounce the oi sound but to hear it. This sound is a unit, treated as one vowel sound. It is usually spelled oi inside a word, and oy at the end of a word, The sound is the same whether spelled oi or oy. Please read with the student:

oil	oiled	oiling	oiler
join	joined	joining	joiner
point	pointed	pointing	pointer
spoil	spoiled	spoiling	spoiler
broil	broiled	broiling	broiler

soil	toying	joy	toiled	toil	hoist
coin	boiling	boy	boiler	foil	point
coil	hoisted	coy	boiled	joint	moist
ploy	hoisting	boil	toiling	foist	enjoy

Please demonstrate the glide and the change in mouth position in pronouncing this diphthong. Please note that the oi (oy) sound is not affected by the addition of the endings ing, er, and ed as are vowels. There is no long or short sound of a diphthong. It is always the same sound.

The EI (EY) Diphthong

This is the least encountered of the diphthongs. It is usually spelled ei within a word and ey at the end of a word. Please note with the student:

rein   veil   vein   their   reindeer

In the above, the diphthong sound resembling long a is heard. For the teacher's information, if letter c precedes the ei, then the ei has the long e sound and is not a diphthong. Examples:

receive   conceive   deceive   perceive   ceiling

This will be explained to the student in a higher level.

The ey spelling of the diphthong is found at the end of a word. Please read with the student:

whey   they   obey   convey   prey

This diphthong sound of ey occurs only when the last syllable of the word is stressed, accentuating the ey. When the ey syllable is unstressed, the ey has a sound like a long e: money   turkey   honey   chimney   journey

Again, this is for the teacher's information only, and will be explained to the student in a higher level.

Please point out the diphthong examples in bold print to the student. It is disconcerting to have similar spellings that can represent sounds that are so different. Again, it will have to be a trial and error approach in getting the proper sound for the printed word. The only reason for introducing this diphthong ey at this point is so that I can use the word <u>they</u> in the Level Two stories.

THE TWO SOUNDS OF LETTER C

In Level One, only the k sound of letter c is used. Letter c is one of the few letters of the alphabet that has a name entirely different from its sounds. The sound ascribed to letter c is either k or s. There is a simple rule to determine which sound to use in any given word:

Before the letters e, i, and y, letter c has the sound of s. In <u>all</u> other situations, it has the k sound. Please read these k sounds of letter c with the student:

can   cat   cut   cot   cop   cap   cub   cup   cob

There are just a few one-syllable words that use the letter c before e, i, or y to get the s sound:

cyst   cell   cent   cede   cinch

Most one-syllable words use the letter s to get the initial s sound, and not the letter c. However, the initial s sound of letter c is common in multiple syllable words:

cinder   cider   cipher   cigar   center   cement
censor   cynic   cellar   civil   citrus   cymbal

If the k sound is desired before the vowels e, i, and y, then the letter k and not the letter c must be used:

kiss   kill   kite   kid   kit   keg   keep   keen
kennel   kettle   kick

This rule that letter c is always a k sound except before vowels e, i, and y is important in multiple syllable words. Please remember that each syllable is a separate unit as far as phonic rules are concerned. One syllable does not influence the preceding or succeeding syllable. Please read the following words with the student to demonstrate that the same word may use the two sounds of letter c, both the k and the s sounds:

circus   cir cus   circle   cir cle   cycle   cy cle
cyclic   cy clic   cyclone   cy clone   cancel   can cel

In the cc combination, the same rule holds: c = s only before e, i, and y. In the word **succeed**, the syllable split occurs between the two c's. However, because they are pronounced differently, there are two sounds, and not one, as is the usual rule with double consonants separating syllables. In the first syllable, **suc**, the syllable ends with the k sound. In the second syllable, **ceed**, the syllable begins with the s sound of c. Please point out this concept to the student in the following words:

accident	succeed	accept	access
occident	succinct	success	accent

In many instances, the cc combination is such that both c's have the same hard sound:

accuse   Mecca   occult   occlude   occupy   succor

In the above list, only one k sound is heard when pronouncing the word, just as in other words with double consonants separating syllables.

Please note that the letter c is not doubled before the endings ing, er, and ed in order to keep the preceding vowel short. The ck combination is used instead.

panic	panicked	panicking	
picnic	picnicker	picnicked	picnicking
frolic	frolicker	frolicked	frolicking
shellac	shellacker	shellacking	shellacked

The reason for this is that a c before the e or i would be pronounced as an s. It is to preserve the k sound that a ck is used instead of a cc before the endings ing, er, and ed.

The s sound of letter c is commonly used to ensure that none of the z sound of s will get into words where the soft s sound is wanted. If the word lace were spelled with an s, and became lase, there would be a temptation to make the s sound hard, like the z sound. It is the same if rice is spelled with an s to get rise. In the spelling rice it is known that the soft s sound is wanted. In the spelling rise it is unclear what is meant.

Some practice words with the s sound of c. Please note that in this case the c is always followed by e, i, or y.

dance	race	spruce	chance	ace	space
since	mice	pencil	prince	ice	slice
fence	lacy	traced	pacing	trace	brace
mince	face	cancer	racing	place	icing
racer	pace	tracer	tracing	slicing	fancy
raced	rice	braced	bracing	dancing	price

THE TWO SOUNDS OF LETTER G

Letter g follows the same rule as does letter c in determining which sound is used, hard or soft. Before the vowels e, i, and y, the letter g takes the soft sound. Otherwise, the sound is hard. Practice with the soft sound:

ginger	gypsy	gentle	page	gym	stage
fringe	badge	sponge	wage	ridge	hedge
plunge	budge	bridge	gender	change	fudge

Some words with the hard sound of letter g:

got	gal	gag	fog	gull	wig	hug	bug
hag	bag	fig	pig	gate	dog	mug	hog

Please note the effect of the silent e on the letter g:

rag rage   hug huge   wag wage   sag sage

Some mixed hard and soft g sounds:

page	change	glass	gene	aggrevate	gadget
game	gallop	hinge	gem	suggest	gamble
gasp	gather	ledge	gym	baggage	gender
glad	ginger	glide	gin	gobble	engine
glut	beggar	globe	god	gloss	gentle
gang	pledge	wage	dog	cage	glider

As in the case of letter c, the g in each syllable is treated separately. The words gadget and baggage have both the hard and soft g sounds.

SUMMARY OF PHONIC RULES
READING LEVEL TWO

1. A syllable is a part of a word pronounced with a single, uninterrupted sounding of the voice. It is a unit of pronunciation, and must contain a vowel. Syllables usually contain one or more consonants, but this is not necessary for a unit to be pronounced. A single vowel alone can be the entire syllable.

2. Syllables usually divide between doubled consonants.

      rab bit   com mit   hap pen   sud den   com mon

However, in rapid speech only one consonant sound is heard for the double consonant, and this goes with the former syllable.

3. Words with two consonants at the syllable break usually divide between the consonants.

   un fit   num ber   nap kin   un der   wel fare   in form

4. In composite words, the syllable split occurs between the words that make up the larger word.

   bath tub   dish pan   tin smith   land lord   base ball

5. When only one consonant occurs at the syllable break, the division depends upon whether or not the first vowel is long or short.

     When the first vowel is pronounced long, the consonant goes with the second syllable.

    si lent   ri val   stu pid   so da   fla vor   bo nus

     When the first vowel is pronounced short, the consonant goes with the first syllable.

    lin en   mod est   vis it   lim it   hab it   riv er

6. A silent e at the end of a word lengthens the sound of the preceding vowel if only one consonant separates the e from that vowel.

       hat hate   bit bite   hop hope   tub tube

This same effect occurs by the addition of the endings ing, er, ed, le, and y.

wipe wiped wiping wiper   bible cradle holy

To prevent this lengthening of the preceding vowel sound, the final consonant must be doubled before the endings ing, er, le, ed, and y.

mud muddy   set settle   hop hopping
bat batted   rob robber

7. A diphthong is a combination vowel sound, made up of two vowel sounds gliding together.

Oi and oy are different spellings for the same diphthong sound, as in words like boil, toil, coin, and boy, joy, toy, and ploy. Ei and ey are different spellings for the same diphthong, as in the words vein, they, and obey. Unlike the oi and oy spellings, which are always the same sound, there are other non-diphthong sounds for the spellings ei and ey.

8. Letter c has no sound of its own. It is always pronounced as a k sound except before the letters e, i, and y, where is is pronounced as an s sound.

cent cell cinch cyst cynic
can cat cut cot cop
circus circle cycle succeed accuse soccer

9. Letter g has both a hard and a soft sound. It follows the same rules as letter c in this regard. Before the vowels e, i, and y, g takes the soft sound. Otherwise, the sound is hard.

ginger gypsy gentle fudge stage wage
got gal gull fog wig hug fig pig

Addition of a silent e converts the g from a hard to a soft sound:

rag rage   hug huge   wag wage

LEVEL TWO STORIES

1.   THE RACE

2.   THE CAMPING TRIP

3.   THE HUT

4.   THE SHIP

Please read these stories with the student and help him with any difficulties. The words are limited to phonic principles covered in Levels One and Two. If there are any problems, please re-do the appropriate exercises.

THE RACE

Robert was the smallest boy in the class.
This mattered just at recess time. Then the kids
picked sides for games. Robert was the last kid
to be picked for a side. Robert was fast and
strong for his size, but the other kids were
faster and stronger, and much bigger. When kids
pick sides for a game of basketball, they need the
biggest kids to have the best chance for winning.

In time, Robert will be just as big as the other kids. His mother is tall. His dad is a big man. Even his brother and his sister got to be big kids. In games that did not use a ball, or make a kid run, Robert did just as well as the bigger kids. Still, Robert was the last kid picked, no matter what the game.

It was almost summer, the time for the big bike race. Robert had not entered this race in the past, as he felt that he had no chance of winning. But this time he had a plan for success. The race was ten miles long. It began on the close side of a big hill, and ended on the other side. The rule was that all the kids began the race at the same place at the same time, and the kid who got to the finish line before the rest was the winner. Robert did not see a rule that made the riders keep on the path. His plan was to take short cuts.

Robert went with his bike along the path of the race the week before. He noted the best places for taking short cuts. The path went back and forth a lot, just to avoid steep and rocky places and the river that went by the hill. These spots used as short cuts saved the most time. The problem was the rocks and thorns that cut his bike tires when he went over them. When he got home, he had his dad put thick tires on his bike. These made the bike less speedy, but it let him take the short cuts and not get flat tires on the pointed edges.

He went over the path a second time, just before the race. He had hidden ropes in the bushes, to use in pulling his bike up most of the steep short cuts. He hid cans of soda along the path. He even made a raft to get across the river with his bike. That raft crossing alone saved three miles.

There was a bit of a drizzle before the race began. It made the paths moist and slippery. When the race began, he let all the other kids get up the path before him. He did not want them to see him taking short cuts. He was used to it, to be the last in line. But this time, it was his plan to be last.

He had placed bushes and shrubs at the short cut spots so the other kids did not see them. It was fun to do what he had planned. He got his rope from the hiding place. He used it to attach to the handles and pull his bike up the steep slopes, places so steep that he was not able to ride up. The rocks and thorns did not cut his thick bike tires. His cans and bottles of soda tasted fine after he got them from the places he had hidden them.

He used the raft to get across the river. The river was not deep, but had a lot of sand on the bottom. Robert did not want to take a chance on getting his bike stuck, and it was better to keep his bike dry. A wet bike will rust the metal. That he did not want.

He did use the path for most of the race. When he noted that another kid was getting close, he went to another short cut. He did not use all the short cuts since they were getting muddy and slippery. He wanted to just win the race, and not be at the finish line a long time before the rest of the kids.

Robert won the race. The gang was a bit puzzled that he was the winner, as they had not suspected that he was so strong. The biggest kid in the class was in second place. The prize was a bucket of candy and a jug of cider. He shared the candy and cider with the other kids. He did not tell them he used short cuts. The kids liked it that he shared the candy with them, and did not pick him last at recess anymore. He was fast, but not big. His size no longer mattered with the other kids, and that made Robert happy indeed.

THE CAMPING TRIP

It was the middle of summer and Danny wanted to go on a camping trip. He did not want to go for a long time, just for the weekend. Whenever he went with his mom and dad, it seemed to be for such a long time that he missed his pals. He wanted to go on a camping trip with just kids, and just for a short time. Then the kids had no mom or dad to boss them.

He got his dad's tent. It was so big that no matter if the whole gang came along on the trip, all had a place to sleep in it. But it was also so big that it did not fit in a backpack. So, Danny put it in his wagon. He wanted to set up camp by the pond, at the place he went fishing. It was the best spot, with lots of shade, and close to the path. It was just a mile from his home.

Almost all the other kids Danny asked to go along with him had other things to do. It was just Bruce and Jack who wanted to go along. Bruce had lots of things that he wanted to bring with him. He wanted to take his stack of comics, and his baseball and bat. Jack wanted to take a lot of cans of soda. He also had a bunch of toys that he wanted to bring. Danny's mom gave them lunches to take along. It was her plan to stop by later and bring along supper for them. The kids planned to have a lot of fish for her to take home when she came with the supper for them.

    The wagon was so full that all three kids had
to push or pull to make it go. After a block, the
kids stopped to drink a soda. Danny's mom had put
the sodas in a small ice chest, and so they tasted
wet and cold. Other kids came over to see what
the three campers had on the wagon. When Sue came
over, she wanted to trade comics. She had not
seen all the comics that Bruce had on the wagon,
and he had not seen those that she had. So, a

trade was made. Ann wanted a drink, and gave the boys a dime for a can of soda. A bunch of other kids did the same, and before long no soda was left.

It did not take long before the whole gang of kids was by the wagon. They began to trade toys. Jack did not want all the toys he had, and traded them for others. Jack had fun spinning the top he got in exchange for a toy truck. Bruce traded a stuffed bunny rabbit for a small toy puppy dog that made a noise when it was petted. Since Bruce had a baseball and bat, why not pick sides and get up a game of baseball? This they did. The boys shared the lunch with the other kids. It was so much fun to do things with a gang of pals that Danny did not want to go on that camping trip after all. It was the same with Bruce and Jack. When it got late and was time for supper, the kids went back home.

Danny's mom had seen that the boys got just to the end of the block. That was O.K. with her. She had not wanted the boys to go on a camping trip, but she let them try it for the fun of it. Supper was on the table when Danny got home. He was happy with the things he got for the things that he gave to the other kids. His mom and dad were glad that he had so much fun. Danny felt that it was like shopping in a store that did not want cash for toys. He was tired of the toys he gave to the other kids and happy with the toys he got back for them. Who wants to go on a camping trip when they can do better things?

THE HUT

Jeff did not like it at all that his little sister went into his closet when he was not at home. That was the place he kept his toys. Her name was Jill. She was seven and he was nine. She had a closet to keep her toys in, but she liked it better to go into his closet. She liked his boy toys better than her dolls. He had lots of gadgets on his toys that made funny noises or made wheels spin. With the push of a button, the fun began. She liked best the space ship with the red dome that began to spin and go up and flash faster and faster until it went off and on so fast that she was not able to see all the blinks. It was much more fun than just putting a dress on a doll. But she often forgot to push the off button, and his battery did not last long with the switch in the on spot. This made him mad. The closets had no locks. He did not want to bother with her toys at all. He wanted her to let his toys alone and never go in his closet. But she went back to his closet whenever he was with his pals.

Jeff and his pals had formed a club. They met in a hut which they had made from bricks and planks and poles and sticks that they put together with rope and cement. It was a place for the boys to meet and not have other kids pester them. It was a place that Jeff did not let his sister in. She was not a member. Just boys had formed the club, and just boys went in the hut.

Jeff had a plan to keep his toys from his sister. It was to take all his toys from his closet and bring them to the hut. Then Jill had no chance to get them when he was not at home. The club was off limits to her. His toys seemed to be safe.

The other members of the club liked his toys. They used them all the time. It was not long before a strap or a string on a toy got broken. Then a clamp on his plane got lost and a wheel fell off. Then a toy got a dent by crashing into a bench. Then the flasher switch got stuck on his truck. This is what happens to toys when kids use them a lot. It was not long before no toy was free of dents, scratches, or missing things. Jeff did not want the kids to use his toys so much. He just wanted the toys to be safe from his sister. It seemed funny to him that it was not his sister who broke his toys, but his pals. All she ever did was let the switch on, which was no problem. The battery just needed a little time in the battery box that put energy back into it and then it was put back into the toy. This was not the case with his pals in the hut. Things got broken all the time. The hut was not such a safe place to keep things after all.

Jeff got his broken toys and put them back in his closet. He wanted his dad to fix them, so he told him the fib that it was his sister Jill who had broken them. His dad fixed them, and put a lock on the closet so that Jill was not able to get in like she used to be able to do. Dad did not spank Jill, as Jeff wanted him to do. Jeff

did not like his sister all that much, as she was such a pest. He did not like to tell his dad that fib but it got all his toys fixed and got a nice lock on his closet.

Jill was mad at Jeff. She had not broken his toys. She told her mom what Jeff did. Mom got a plan to see which of the kids was telling the truth, Jeff or Jill. Mom sent Jeff to the store to get a bottle of milk for her. Then she went to the hut to ask the kids what had happened to the toys. They told her the truth, that they had broken them while using them so much at the hut. She gave the club members a bag of candy. The boys liked the snack. She was glad that the boys had told her the truth and had not joined in the lie that Jeff made up. She was mad at Jeff for telling them such a fib. When Jeff got home from the store, she made him tell his dad the truth. Jeff had to tell Jill that he was sorry that he had made up such a big fib.

His mom and dad did not keep mad at him. Jeff had to do more jobs at home for a week. But after that, they forgot the whole thing. If any toys got broken, dad fixed them. It did not matter who broke them. Jill gave Jeff a gadget that she got in the store. It just needed to be plugged in and then wired to a toy so that a battery was not needed. After awhile, Jeff stopped using the lock on his closet. It was O.K. with him if Jill used his toys. After all, she was careful and never broke them.

THE SHIP

David was Peter's best pal, and Peter was David's best pal. This was so since the second grade, a long time ago. When David came to Peter's home, he often spent so much time with him that he ate both lunch and supper with Peter. It was the same when Peter went to David's home. They acted like brothers.

David's mom and dad had planned a trip for a long time. It was a trip on a ship, and was to last for a whole month. David had to go along with them. He had no choice but to obey the wishes of his parents. He did not want to be on a ship for so long a time. He wanted to just be at home and spend time with his pal Peter.

The boys made a plan. Peter was to go along with David and his mom and dad to the ship, to see David off on his trip. The plan was for Peter to get on the ship, and hide. David's mom and dad did not plan to be in the cabin much of the time. Mom planned to spend much of her time just sitting on the deck of the ship and getting a suntan. Dad planned to do lots of swimming and spend time at tennis. It was such a big ship that the pals had many places to go and not run the risk of bumping into David's mom and dad. Both boys wore the same size clothing, and it was the boys' plan for David to share his clothes with Peter. David had taken a lot of extra things in his baggage so that he had plenty to share with Peter.

Peter did go along to the dock, to see David off on his trip. When he had the chance, Peter snuck on the ship and hid under the bunk in David's cabin. The cabin was small, but nice. David put a blanket and other bedding under the bunk for Peter. Peter had left a note at his home for his mom and dad. It told them what he did, and why. He did not want to be alone and not see his pal for a whole month. By the time they got the note, no time was left to stop him.

A huge crane put the luggage on the deck, the gangplank was hoisted, and the ship left the dock. Peter and David began to inspect the entire ship. The ship had three upper decks. The boilers were deep in the hull, and the noise that they made was just a whisper on the upper levels. The ship had a big dining hall. It had stores. It had snack tables. It had a game hall. It had a gym. It even had a T.V. hall with a lot of T.V. sets and a shelf filled with cassettes of many of the latest programs.

The boys spent time watching T.V. and enjoying the games in the game hall. When they felt like it, they went to a snack table. David made a point of visiting his mom and dad on the deck for a short time while Peter hid in the game hall or on the upper deck. Then the boys met and went off to do other things.

The boys planned to sleep in the same bed. Peter was to keep hidden under David's bed until after his mom and dad got to sleep. Then it was safe to get into bed with David until it was time to get up, and then Peter had to hide under the bed until David's mom and dad left. That was the plan they had made up. They felt that it was to be a big success. But when the boys got back to the cabin, they noted that another bunk was in the cabin. It was a small bed, the same size as David's.

David went into the cabin to see what was happening. David's dad had hidden in the small closet on the other side of the hall. He wanted to catch the boys together. Peter went in the

cabin after David waved to him that it was safe.
Then David's dad came in the cabin after them.
Peter did not try to run. On a ship he had no
chance to escape. David's dad told the boys that
Peter's mom and dad had sent a message to the
skipper to inform him that Peter was on the ship.
They also sent a check to the ship's address in
the city for Peter's passage. Peter's dad was mad

that Peter had hidden on the ship, but he did not want Peter hiding all the time. As long as Peter was along with them on the ship, he was to have fun. This made the boys very happy.

The rest of the trip was a lot of fun for the boys. When Peter got home, his mom and dad did not seem to be mad at him. They did not like the trick that Peter did, but did not plan to punish him. Peter's mom and dad had decided to take a trip to France, a trip that they had wanted to go on for a long time. They enjoyed the trip very much. They felt much better after getting back. It was a nice event for all of them, and they did not want to spoil such a nice, fun-filled summer by getting mad. But the dads of both boys told them that they had better not ever plan to do any more things like they did this summer. If they did, they had better also plan on a spanking, which no kid wants.

READING LEVEL THREE

Involving Vowels –
More and Less Vocal

THE LONG SOUND OF LETTER A

There is a general rule that whenever two vowels are present in the same syllable, the first will be pronounced long and the second is silent. Please remember that there can be only one vowel sound in a syllable. This is mandated by the definition of a syllable. If one wants to sound two vowels, then two separate syllables must result.

In Level One, the long vowel sound was indicated by the addition of a "silent e" to the end of the word (syllable): rat-rate, hat-hate. In this level, the long vowel sound is indicated by the addition of a second vowel immediately following the first. This second vowel is not pronounced.

Letter a is often given the long vowel sound by the addition of the letter i:

ran rain   pan pain   man main   van vain

Some practice words with the ai combination:

wait	chain	aim	Cain	saint	laid
maid	braid	bait	drain	faith	tail
pain	train	mail	faint	saint	sail
gait	snail	hail	frail	brain	rail
jail	trail	gail	paint	faith	gain
bait	plain	pail	faint	train	wail
main	stain	paid	grain	strain	bail

At the end of words, this ai combination is spelled ay:

lay	say	bray	pay	play	slay	stay
hay	gay	sway	ray	tray	spray	pray
may	day	clay	bay	flay	stray	gray

There is a reason for these two different ways of producing the long a sound. Originally, the sound of a in the word hate and the sound of a in the word pain were different. The ai of pain was pronounced like a diphthong. With the evolution of the language, the diphthongs tended to disappear and to be replaced by the single long vowel sound.

THE LONG SOUND OF LETTER O

The vowel o usually lengthens by the addition of letter a, giving the oa combination for the sound of long o. This second vowel, the a, is silent.

cot coat   rod road   Tod toad

Some practice oa words:

soap	float	throat	boat	moat	oar	coat
loaf	toast	coach	load	road	oak	goal
toad	roast	coast	oath	loan	foal	coal
moan	croak	groan	soak	foam	roam	oats
coax	cocoa	boast	soar	roar	boar	whoa

The "silent e" can be added next to the o, without a consonant in between, giving the oe combination to produce the long o sound:

foe   toe   doe   woe   hoe   Joe

The letter w can sometimes take on the qualities of a vowel. Indeed, the w is a <u>double u</u>. It is therefore not surprising that the letter w can function as the second, silent vowel that makes the first vowel long. Thus, the ow combination can be pronounced as a long o, with the w silent:

mow	sow	bowl	grown	fellow	blow	flow
tow	bow	grow	blown	mellow	shown	crow
low	row	slow	flown	bellow	throw	glow

The teacher will know that bow used in the above list means bow as in bow and arrow, and not bow as when referring to a part of a ship. The bow of a ship uses the diphthong form of ow, and will be taken up in the next level.

The consonant letter l lengthens the o when combined with d, t, or l, to give the combinations of ld, lt, or ll. Please note:

fold	mold	cold	hold	stroll	old	colt
sold	told	bolt	dolt	revolt	jolt	gold
volt	roll	molt	toll	scold	poll	bold

In the above situation, the o is lengthened automatically in preparation for pronouncing the l. For fun, try to pronounce the above words with a short o. It is almost impossible, and the resulting word lacks enough vowel sustaining sound to be understandable. This same principle of lengthening a vowel to make it more understandable is found in words like these:

host   post   most   ghost   both

THE DOUBLE O (OO) SOUND

The addition of a second o does not give a long o sound, but forms an entirely new sound. This oo sound has two possible pronunciations, long and short.

Examples of the long oo sound:

broom	roof	stoop	spool	mood	zoo	moon
droop	hoop	stool	booth	hoof	too	cool
troop	loop	drool	brood	root	shoot	soon
stoop	boot	spoon	spoof	room	tooth	fool
moose	tool	goose	loose	toot	smooth	pool

Examples of the short oo sound:

wood	good	hook	foot	hood	blood
cook	soot	look	took	brook	stood
wool	nook	rook	book	flood	shook

There are subtle differences in many of the oo word pronunciations, especially between such words as blood and wood. Nevertheless, these two words are both pronounced more like a short oo sound than a long oo sound. Also, there are marked regional differences in pronunciation of the short oo sound. Because of this, and the desire to avoid a host of sub-classifications, blood (blud) and wood (wud) have both been put into the same general classification.

Rarely, the oo acts as a single o sound, usually before the letter r: door   floor

THE OU COMBINATION

The letter u, when added to the letter o in order to give the combination ou, doesn't automatically create just a long oo or a short oo sound. There are in fact a total of six different possible ways of pronouncing the ou combination. These will all be explained in the next level. However, for the purpose of using the conditional mode in the Level Three stories, the short oo sound for the spelling ou will be introduced now. Please note:

could   would   should

These have the same sound of oo found in words like hood and stood. Please explain to the student that the ou in these words is pronounced as the short sound of oo.

THE LONG E SOUND

In Level One, it was explained that the addition of a "silent e" to an initial e made the first e sound long: met-meet, ten-teen. This same effect can be achieved by the addition of the letter a, giving the ea combination. The result is the same long e sound, even though a different spelling is used. Words that are spelled differently but sound alike are called homonyms. Some homonym pairs:

meet	meat	week	weak	seem	seam	deer	dear
beet	beat	peel	peal	peek	peak	flee	flea
teem	team	steel	steal	feet	feat	seel	seal

These words have exactly the same sound. Hearing them, one cannot tell which word (meaning) is intended except when the word is in the context of a sentence. However, because the spelling is different, there is no doubt as to which meaning of the word is intended when reading the word. Originally, the ea sound was pronounced like a diphthong, and it was audibly distinguished from the ee sound. With the simplification of pronunciation, these sounds became the same long e sound.

Some practice with long e sounds:

keep	peach	veal	sweet	speech	steam	seat
weed	sheep	beam	sheet	scream	seek	peep
bean	speak	free	sweep	screen	tree	bead
beak	yeast	seal	three	preach	heat	leaf
heap	wheel	weep	teach	stream	need	seed
keep	dream	keel	green	stream	tea	seen
feed	clear	reap	cheat	beast	bee	neat
lean	creep	deep	cheap	beach	see	leap
feel	wheat	east	greet	reach	wee	beep

The e at the end of a short word is usually the long sound:

me   be   she   he   we

THE EI AND IE COMBINATIONS

The ei and ie combinations are pronounced the same, as a long e. However, in our rigid spelling system, it matters how the combination appears in a word. Although the sound is exactly the same, one combination is right for certain words, and the other way is right for other words. The general rule states: i before e, except after c.

Examples of the ie combination for the long e sound:

field	believe	bier	thief	shield
yield	achieve	chief	fierce	shriek
grief	relieve	fiend	apiece	priest
brief	hygiene	siege	pierce	diesel
piece	mischief	niece	relief	belief

After c, this long e sound combination is spelled ei:

ceiling	conceive	deceive	receipt
receive	perceive	deceit	conceit

The rule states, in its entirety: <u>i before e, except after c or when pronounced like a, as in neighbor and weigh.</u> The latter is the diphthong form of ei, introduced in the previous level. Some examples of the diphthong form:

vein	beige	sleigh	weigh
veil	their	neighbor	reign

The silent gh of neighbor, etc. will be taken up in the next level. It is not necessary to explain this to the student at this time.

Of course, with most rules, there are exceptions. Some exceptions to the above spelling rule:

protein	weird	either	neither
foreign	seize	caffeine	forfeit

The main point of this discussion is that a second vowel in a syllable usually makes the first vowel long. In the case of letter e, the second vowel can be another e, an a, or an i. With the i, the inverted spelling somehow got started and then frozen into the language. Only rarely is another vowel used to lengthen the e, such as the o in the word **people.**

THE LONG I SOUND

The long i sound in a syllable is achieved by the addition of an e, or by changing the i to y, usually at the end of a word:

pie   die   tie   lie

(In longer words, the ie usually takes the long e sound.)

cry	why	shy	sky	fly
dry	sly	try	by	fry

In multiple-syllable words, the i achieves the long sound by its placement at the end of an accentuated syllable:

bicycle	pilot	tidings	biceps	viper	final
microbe	dilate	migrate	silent	pica	libel

There are two consonant groups that usually lengthen the i sound. These are the nd and ld combinations:

blind   mind   kind   bind   find   hind

grind   mild   wild   wind   child

The i usually has the long sound before the silent gh, which will be taken up in the next level. Some examples for now:

night   flight   sight   fight   might   light

THE LONG U SOUND

The vowel u can attain the long sound by the addition of e, thus producing the ue combination:

| argue | sue | cue | Tuesday | glue | blue |
| value | hue | due | continue | rescue | true |

The addition of i to u, giving the ui combination, gives the long u sound:

| fruit | nuisance | suit | bruise |
| juice | cruise | juicy | suitor |

Rarely, the uu combination is used to lengthen the u, as in the word **vacuum.**

This section of Level Three has been concerned with ways in which the reader can tell whether a vowel sound is to be pronounced long or short. It would be wonderful if there were rules with no exceptions. However, a rule that works 90% of the time is better than no rule at all. It is by the irregularities and subtleties of a language that the native speaker may be distinguished from the foreigner. This is what gives an individual his sense of superiority concerning his native language. One begins to regard irregularities with more tolerance once they have been mastered. Anyone who has become fluent in a foreign language will attest to this.

THE SCHWA

In everyday speech there is a tendency to reduce words to the essential sounds needed for understanding. Excess sounds become de-emphasized or are dropped altogether.

When vowel sounds are minimized in sound value to the point of being nearly, but not quite, dropped, the resulting sound is called a <u>schwa</u>. The schwa is a sound that does not sound exactly like any of the vowels but replaces the vowel in unaccentuated syllables. This de-emphasized sound is the same for all vowels: a, e, i, o, and u. The schwa is the sound in:

<u>a</u>go　it<u>e</u>m　san<u>i</u>ty　butt<u>o</u>n　foc<u>u</u>s

The dictionary symbol for the schwa is (ə). Inspection of any page in a dictionary and glancing over the pronunciation symbols will reveal a very high percentage of schwa vowels. The schwa sound is a major reason why poor readers are poor spellers. Frequently, words cannot be spelled as they sound because of this schwa effect. No clue is given as to what vowel is in the word because all vowels sound alike when reduced to the schwa level. The only hint as to where one might find a schwa sound is that it occurs frequently in unaccentuated syllables of multiple-syllable words. In addition, it is often found in some of our most commonly used mono-syllable words. This is why students will write dun for done and sum for some. The poor reader will not have noticed that the o vowel in done and some is not the long o of lone and stone, but a deemphasized vowel, the schwa. Some examples of the schwa:

Schwa a:

central	normal	total	beta	final	pedal
climate	signal	metal	drama	local	arena
algebra	cinema	cellar	gamma	dogma	delta

Schwa e:

| tunnel | nickel | hunger | lender | bushel |
| blister | chatter | slender | thunder | glider |

Schwa o:

| doctor | harbor | favor | color | terror |
| cannon | tractor | labor | motor | factor |

Schwa i:

| caliber | domino | bird | dirt | edible | unity |
| justice | engine | girl | firm | alibi | mirth |

Schwa u:

| fungus | minus | focus | chorus | virus | campus |

How does one determine when a vowel is a schwa sound? One can tell only by trying it. If **done** is pronounced with a long o, it rhymes with **bone.** This is not a recognizable word. The next thing to try is the schwa, which sounds like "dun" and is a recognizable sound corresponding to a word the reader knows. It is surprising how soon this becomes an automatic response. The schwa is an important concept in teaching reading, and will be taken up again later.

Why does English have a schwa sound? To better understand the schwa concept, one has to realize that people can think faster than they are able to speak. The schwa is a way to speed up spoken communication. Vowels take time to be uttered, and the less value assigned to a vowel, the faster it can be spoken. In an unemphasized syllable, it is not necessary to put all that effort into sounding out the vowel when the hearer already understands the word from the other syllables. Thus, the schwa is a form of linguistic shorthand, a way of getting spoken information transmitted faster. If students are made aware of the schwa concept early, they will pay more attention to unaccentuated syllables and save countless hours later on when they are able to avoid tedious spelling drill.

LETTER R AND THE SCHWA

There are three consonants that can have a profound effect on a preceding vowel. They are r, l, and w. Letters r and l are classified as "liquids" because they are the only consonants that are nonfrictional when pronounced. Letter w is classified as a semivowel. In Level Three, only the r is discussed concerning this effect on preceding vowels.

The weak vowels are e, i, and u. Before the consonant r, which is formed in the front part of the mouth, the 'weak' vowels e, i, and u are reduced to the schwa sound. Please read the list below with the student and note that the **er, ir,** and ur spellings are all sounded the same.

The ER, IR, and UR Combinations:

perch	churn	girl	hurl	murmur	sir	herd
birch	lurch	firm	fern	church	fur	stir
twirl	skirt	stir	purr	thirst	her	curb
berth	birch	hurt	burn	clerk	dirt	turn
first	shirk	surf	burn	churn	spur	bird
whirl	burst	furl	curl	shirt	whir	jerk

The OR Combination

In the or combination, the schwa effect on the vowel o is not complete, as the o is the strongest vowel when sounded. The o sound is somewhat modified by the r, but it is still distinctly sounded as an o.

torch	stork	fort	sort	port	for	horn
thorn	porch	cord	form	lord	storm	corn
sworn	stork	born	pork	cork	sport	sort
short	north	cork	worn	fork	scorch	torn

The AR Combination

Before letter r, the schwa effect on a is not complete, since a, like o, is a strong vowel. The a sound in ar is not like the short or long a sound but is still recognizable as a vowel sound of a.

start	dark	lard	darn	car	bar
shark	hard	farm	yard	par	arm
marsh	star	park	bark	jar	tar
smart	spark	scar	darn	art	ark
chart	scarf	cart	lark	mar	far

There is a situation where the ar sound is modified by an initial w, giving the **war** combination that is pronounced <u>wor</u>. In this situation, the w causes the a in the ar to take on the sound of the short o. Please note:

warm	warned	war	warn
warp	warrenty	wart	ward

The effect of the w on the ar is subtle and need not be drilled excessively with the student at this time. It is caused by the effect of the semi-vowel character of w on the partial schwa sound in the ar combination. Such a sound is too weak a vowel sound to carry a characteristically distinctive sound, and a shift of vowel to the posterior, rounded o sound was noted as far back as the Anglo-Saxon period of the development of the English language.

Please note that the letter r can have the schwa effect only on short vowels. It has little or no effect on long vowels. This rule holds no matter how the vowel is lengthened, whether by the addition of a succeeding vowel or by a "silent e" at the end of the syllable.

Long Vowels and the Schwa:

fir	fire	sir	sire	bar	bare		curb	cure
par	pair	her	here	dirt	dire		curl	cure
far	fair	car	care	dark	dare		purr	pure
scar	scare		star	stare	stair	hard	hair	hare

hire	chore	wire	dear	air	gear
year	snore	more	wore	sore	fear
core	store	cheer	fare	pair	bore
boar	steer	chair	cure	near	peer

As with all rules, there are exceptions. A noteable one is the word **were**. It rhymes with **her** instead of rhyming with **here**. Some other non-law-abiding words are **some** and **done,** having a short schwa-quality vowel sound rather than a full long o vowel sound that should obey the "silent e" rule. It is the same situation with the word **have**. It should rhyme with **rave** and **brave**. It is frequently the very common words that violate the rules. However, because these words are very common and therefore frequently encountered, they are quickly learned and will present no problem for the student who reads frequently.

The schwa (ə) is a very important concept in teaching reading. Just a note about pronunciation marks: there are many pronunciation symbols in the dictionary to indicate the sound of a word. Phonetics is the name of the science that deals with the recording of speech sounds by the use of symbols. Many reading books use special markings, such as diacritical marks, to indicate the proper pronunciation of words. This book, however, is about phonics. Phonics is simplified phonetics for the purpose of teaching reading, and uses none of the phonetician's devices. Those special markings can be of value after the student has learned basic reading, but they tend to hinder more than they help the beginning reader and the author has elected to omit them from this book. After all, there are no pronunciation marks in everyday reading material.

UNSTRESSED ENDINGS

In speech, verbs tend to have stressed endings while nouns tend to have unstressed endings. In the case of verbs, the endings carry a lot of information regarding the person and tense and have to be clearly heard by the listener. This is especially evident in words that are both nouns and verbs. Please contrast the following sentences: (1) He is a reb'el. (2) If they don't get better food soon the prisoners will rebel'.

This section of Level Three is concerned with unstressed endings of nouns. These unstressed endings usually contain schwa vowel sounds and tend to sound alike. There is a tendency for lazy readers to pay the greatest attention to the beginning of a word and let the end of the word go by with only cursory attention. Such readers tend to guess the ending without actually noting the letters. Indeed, this technique is actually taught by the proponents of "whole word" recognition. Such teachers encourage the student to note the first letter of a word and the approximate length, and then guess its meaning. Absolutely nothing could be more destructive to learning to read than this technique. The student must be taught to pay attention to all the letters and not slough off the final part of a word just because so many endings sound the same. Only by noting all the letters can a student learn to spell properly.

Endings ER, OR, and AR

Please note the schwa effect of these unstressed endings. They all sound very much alike.

motor	color	trailer	glider	doctor
sailor	labor	slender	harbor	hunger
favor	eager	thunder	mirror	dealer
cellar	humor	chatter	blister	parlor
terror	error	tractor	similar	nectar
editor	major	calendar	regular	horror

The following are words that are much more difficult than heretofore presented. Please read them with the student to demonstrate that the endings, although spelled differently, are pronounced the same because they are unstressed syllables. It is not necessary that the student understand these words, or even study them.

Words Ending in AIN, AN, IN, INE, ION, ON
These tend to sound alike:

pardon	cabin	captain	region	curtain
raisin	human	champion	margin	genuine
ribbon	organ	religion	person	Britain
engine	robin	chaplain	carton	bargain
carbon	melon	chieftain	imagine	certain

Words Ending in LE, EL, AL
These tend to sound alike:

pickle	grumble	final	puzzle	animal
nozzle	central	local	single	saddle
riddle	carnival	metal	musical	normal
nickel	personal	total	chuckle	signal
shovel	struggle	level	eternal	tunnel
bushel	tropical	needle	medical	weasel

Words Ending in ET, IT, OT, ATE, and UTE.
These tend to sound alike:

pilot	minute	climate	socket	unit	credit
limit	carrot	deposit	spirit	orbit	nugget
visit	parrot	scarlet	private	hermit	gadget

Words Ending in ABLE and IBLE
These tend to sound alike:

sensible	irritable	edible	dependable
flexible	flammable	probable	incredible
eligible	responsible	favorable	deplorable
portable	predictable	invisible	believable
terrible	inflammable	available	impossible

Words Ending in ANCE and ENCE
These tend to sound alike:

innocence	deliverance	absence	appearance
tolerance	performance	residence	confidence
abundance	intelligence	annoyance	importance
ignorance	independence	providence	attendance

The above words are more for the teacher's edification than for the student's instruction. The point is that unstressed endings that are similar except for a different vowel, which has a schwa sound, tend to sound alike. It is important that the student examine every letter when encountering a new word, including the ending, even if he knows or guesses its meaning before completing a scan of the entire word. The endings must be noticed before they can be learned and spelled properly. This attention will not slow down the student when he becomes a proficient reader. Indeed, it will help him to read even faster. The process is much like learning to play the piano and reading the music. Chords have to be broken down into notes when first encountered. Then, on subsequent encounters, they tend to be recognized immediately. The parts are automatically synthesized into the whole, and the student can tell the teacher what notes are in the chord without having to analyze it specifically once it has been learned consciously. This allows rapid sight reading of new music. The analogy is apt for reading words. Patterns and associations are recognized, and the reading proceeds at a fast pace. If one resorts to guessing, there will be lots of mistakes in meanings of words, and sentences will often make no sense at all. This will require a re-reading of the material, with a consequent overall result of inefficient and slow reading.

The Three Spellings of To

Words that sound alike but are spelled differently are called homonyms (homo = same and nym = name. Thus homonym = same name). The words to, too, and two are commonly confused for the reason that they sound alike but have different meanings. They sound alike for different phonic reasons:

Too has the long double o (oo) sound heard in words like moon and soon. It has the meaning of addition, synonymous with also; for example: me, too.

Two is a number. In Late Middle English, (about 1500), the letter w tended to be silent when preceded by another consonant and followed by a posterior rounded vowel (e.g. sword). Modern pronunciation has restored the w sound in many but not all words containing letter w. This wo sound is indistinguishable from the oo sound as pronounced above.

To is a preposition. Prepositions represent relationships between entities, and to represents motion from the subject toward an object such as going to school. It can be used in the infinitive sense of doing something without limits (in = not and finite = limit), such as going out to play, in which the meaning of infinitive refers to the lack of limits placed upon the word by case endings. Phonically, to should rhyme with go and so, but it is a deemphasized sound, much like the word do. The three homonyms of the sound to (to, too, and two) are so different that the context is sufficient to differentiate which meaning of the sound is indicated. The deemphasized sound to is helpful in achieving more rapid speech, as to is a very common preposition.

LEVEL THREE MISCELLANEOUS

The Letter Q

The letter q is never found alone in English, nor in any European languages based upon Latin. It is always found in the qu combination. The combination qu is pronounced like the combination kw or, rarely, like the letter k alone. Thus, letter q is redundant, as is the qu combination. Qu could easily be replaced by the kw combination as is often seen in advertisements: kwick for quick. Some practice with the qu combination:

queen	quart	quality	quit	squeak	quote
quick	quilt	quarter	quiz	quantum	quite
quake	quart	quarrel	squash	banquet	quill
quack	quail	request	require	quantity	quash

Please remember that the w is really a double u. Thus, it is not surprising that the u of qu takes on a w sound.
In some words the qu has the sound of k alone. This is because the w is often dropped in unemphasized syllables.

antique   plaque   mosquito

The Letter X

The letter x, like the letter c, does not have a sound of its own. Most commonly, x has the sound of ks as in:

mix	extend	explain	ax	extra	hex
fox	expert	exchange	oxen	excuse	six
fix	excite	exchange	axle	express	box

Letter x also has the sound of gz when it is followed by a vowel or by a silent h:

exact   exhaust   exist   exit   exhale   exhort
exude   example   exult   exam   exhibit   exhume

The reason for these two pronunciations of letter x is explained on page 236, in Level Five.

The alphabet has 26 letters, but three of them are superfluous. Letter c is pronounced as either k or s. Q, as it is always used in the qu combination, is readily replaced with kw. The letter x is easily replaced with ks or gz. Letters are representative of sounds, and the letters c, x, and q could be eliminated without any loss of ability to reproduce the sounds they represent.

SUMMARY OF READING LEVEL THREE
PHONIC RULES

1.   Whenever two vowels occur together in the same syllable, the first is usually pronounced long and the second is silent.
 ran rain   cot coat   blue   true   pie die   meet meat

2.   The combinations ei and ie are usually pronounced as a long e sound.
        field   priest   either   neither   ceiling   deceive
The exception to the above is when ei is used as a diphthong, as in the words vein, neighbor, and weigh.

3.   The consonant combinations of nd and ld usually cause the i to take the long sound.
             mind   kind   find   mild   wild   child

4.   The oo sound is not a long o sound, but an entirely new sound, pronounced either long or short.
        Long oo sound: room   roof   stoop   mood   boot   tool
        Short oo sound: good   wood   foot   look   took   book

5.   The schwa is a deemphasized vowel sound in an unaccentuated syllable. It is the vowel sound in: ago, item, sanity, button, and focus.

6.   Before letter r, the weaker vowels e, i, and u form the schwa sound.
        girl   herd   hurl   sir   fur   her   perch   birch   lurch
    The above sounds of er, ir, and ur all sound alike because the vowels e, i, and u have become schwa sounds before the letter r. However, if the syllable ends with a "silent e", there is no schwa sound.
        fir fire   sir sire   her here   dirt dire   curb cure

7.   The combinations or and ar form a semi-schwa sound:
             art   car   bar   hard   for   fort   storm   cork
    The ar and or sounds still have the qualities of the a

and o sounds and are not complete schwa sounds. A "silent e" eliminates this semi-schwa effect.

    sir sire car care bar bare   store chore tore

8.   Long vowel sounds before letter r do not take on the schwa sound.

    par pair far fair   near peer year boar lair

9.   Vowels in unstressed word endings take on the schwa sound, making the endings sound alike regardless of the vowels.

ar, er, or:

color   glider   dealer   error   cellar   slender   cabin

in, ine, ion, on, ain, an:

cabin   certain   organ   raisin   region   carbon   imagine

al, el, le:

pickle   animal   nickel   shovel   total   puzzle   final

et, in, ot, ate, ute:

pilot   minute   visit   carrot   private   nugget   deposit

able, ible:

flexible   probable   edible   portable   possible   capable

ance, ence:

residence   tolerance   appearance   innocence   persistence

11.   To, too, and two sound alike. Too has the double oo sound of moon and soon. Two has the same sound because the w functions as a u (double u) and the ou combination can have the same double o (oo) sound. To has a deempahsized semi-schwa sound and is pronounced the same as too and two.

12.   Letter q is never found alone. It is always followed by u, and has the sound of kw.

    queen quick quart banquet squash quiz

13.   Letter x has no sound of its own. It usually has the sound of ks in words like mix, hex, explain, and extend. When x is followed by a vowel or a silent h, x takes on the sound of gz as in exact, exude, exhort, exhaust and example.

LEVEL THREE STORIES

1. THE FLUTE

2. A BIRTHDAY PARTY

3. THE PICNIC

4. THE CHESS CHAMP

These stories contain words that have phonic aspects explained in Levels One, Two, and Three. If the student has any difficulties, please refer back to the appropriate section and re-do the explanations and drills. The vocabulary is expanded, and help may be required for the student to understand the meanings of some of the words.

THE FLUTE

Janet had a flute. It was long and shiny, and had a very nice tone when played. She had gotten it from an old chest in the attic. It had been her dad's. He had played it in the school band as a teenager, and had it since then. He did not want to play it anymore as he did not have time to practice, and could produce only squeeky notes. When Janet expressed an interest in studying music, he gave it to her. He felt it was a good thing for a girl to learn to play.

Janet liked the flute so much that she kept it with her most of the time. She began taking lessons from the man who played with the city band. She practiced a lot, and was quite happy with the progress she was making.

Janet's little sister Betty was not happy. She did not like it that Janet had something that she did not have. So Betty began to pester Janet whenever she played her flute. She rattled the dishes, banged her toys, slammed doors, and dropped things. She took her toy broom and used it to sweep the floor next to Janet. She squeezed her toy duck to make it quack. She did anything that disturbed. Sometimes she would even put a whole bar of soap into water and stir it to make a thick soapy foam so that she could use a wire loop to blow bubbles that drifted in front of Janet to

keep her from seeing the music. Betty's plan was to be a secret pest, and annoy Janet so that she would quit learning to play the flute. Then Betty could get it and have it all to herself.

Janet kept on with her music. She made such good progress that her dad gave her a reward. It was a bigger case for the flute, made of plastic with a nice handle. Betty got so desperate that she started to turn on the T.V. and the vacuum cleaner whenever Janet was practicing.

Betty decided to ask her dad for her own flute. Betty did not really want to play the flute as much as she wanted Janet to quit. Her dad suspected this and got her a cheap metal flute that was in a wooden case. Betty took her flute from its case and played only when Janet was practicing, really to be the worst pest and annoy her. It seemed that the only way to keep Betty away was to get far away from her. It was useless to try to get mom or dad to scold Betty. She would simply find other ways to do her tricks if told to stop some act. Janet had to go to the garage to avoid a quarrel and to have a single minute's peace from Betty's noise and mischief. It was cool in the garage, but at least it was peaceful. Janet used her dad's tools to make herself a stool from the pile of wood that was in a neat stack in the corner. She took the best pieces of wood and put them together with some nails and then put her blue pillow on top to make a soft seat. Janet was pleased that she could get so much done in such a brief time.

Then something happened that changed Betty's attitude. The city band was all set to give a concert in the city park when Janet's teacher got sick. He was too ill to play in the concert, and called Janet to ask her to take his place. The music on the program contained some important solos for the flute, and the band could not play the music properly with no flute player. It was too late for them to get other music that did not contain parts for the flute in time for the performance.

Janet took her teacher's place, and played very well. The whole family was excited and went to the concert, and they were very impressed with the way Janet played. So were the other members of the band. They invited her to join the band. Her teacher had felt for a long time that the band could use another flute player. Betty was impressed that it was her sister who sat up on the stage and played.

Betty stopped her pestiness. She wanted to hear Janet play, and not have her go to the garage to practice. Soon, Janet was giving flute lessons to her sister. Dad took Betty's flute to the music store and exchanged it for a better flute. Betty practiced a lot, and hoped to soon be as good as her sister, and to someday sit next to her in the city band. After all, if two flute players are good for a band, adding a third should be even better.

A BIRTHDAY PARTY

Soon Doris would have her tenth birthday. She looked forward to her birthday party all year. Her parents let the Birthday Child be the boss for the entire day. They even had a big hat for her to put on, and called her the queen for a day. All other members of the family were her slaves, and had to take orders from the queen. They were not really slaves; they pretended to be so just for fun.

Doris had more girl friends than boy friends. This was the way she wanted it. Boys played mean tricks like pulling her hair and putting bugs on her neck. Girls played nice games like hopscotch and dolls. So, Doris sent cards for her party to many more girls than boys. Her mother wanted her to invite every child in the class, but there were some boys that Doris could not stand. Since it was her party, and she was boss for a day, she did not invite a lot of the boys in the village.

After she mailed the cards, some of the kids got mad when they were not invited. Doris did not care. Her mother did not agree with her, but that is the way mothers are. Mothers don't think the way kids do, and just don't understand that pests are not welcome at a birthday party.

The boys who were not invited to the party had a plan to get even with Doris for the insult.

Other kids teased them for not getting a card to the party, and they were annoyed that they were excluded. They gathered up a bunch of things that Doris hated and put them in boxes of different sizes. Then they covered the boxes with nice party paper and put a big ribbon on each. Some of the ribbons were yellow, some blue, some purple. The packages looked like nice presents.

Then the boys sneaked up to Doris' home and put the presents on her doorstep. After ringing the doorbell, they ran and hid in the bushes. Doris was surprised to find so many presents on her doorstep and quite puzzled that no child was there with them. The boys watched her take them inside, just as they planned that she would do.

The kids who were invited to the party began arriving soon afterwards. Each of them had a present for Doris. Doris greeted each child at the door, wearing her red birthday hat. The boys had been to her party last year, and stayed in the bushes to watch the fun. Doris always opened her presents first, before any games were played. She just could not wait to see what her friends had given her.

Doris began opening presents with the boxes that were left on her doorstep. She could find no cards on the boxes, and wanted to see what was inside. She opened the large pink box first. Then there was a scream. The boys had put a snake in that box. It was just a harmless grass snake, but it scared most of the kids. Doris' dad had to take it away. Doris was quite scared but she

wanted her party to be a success, and pretended
that nothing had happened. She opened the second
box, the one that had a black ribbon over white
paper. There was another scream. This box was
filled with frogs, and they jumped all over the
living room. The boys who were at the party got
them back in the box quickly, and then put the lid
on. Doris' dad put that box in the garage, and
put a big board on the top of the lid so that it
could not come off. This time, she was really
scared, and it was hard to keep her fear a secret
and pretend to be brave. She was worried that her
party would be a flop but went on opening
presents. This time, tho, she opened a present

with a nametag. It had a comic book and a yo-yo inside. That made her feel a lot better. But the next box was different. It had three mice inside. This time even her mother screamed. Doris was lucky that her cat was in the room, and chased the mice away.

This last trick made her parents concerned over what was in the other presents. They moved the party to the back yard and set up tables on the grass. This was what the uninvited boys wanted. They were able to reach from the bushes and get things from the table, like cake and cookies. They were only interested in the food, and not in playing any party games. Their tricks had worked just as they planned, and they got to eat all the food they wanted. They felt that they had gotten even with Doris for not inviting them.

Doris' mother suspected what had happened, that those trick presents were from the boys that had not been invited. Doris agreed. Next year, all the kids were to get cards to her party. Then maybe there would be no more tricks like these, and the party would be just like Doris wanted.

THE PICNIC

It would soon be the day for the class picnic. The students called it Spring Play Day as it was held either the first or second weekend in April. The teachers liked having the picnic, as they were able to get more work from the students. It was a rule that just the students with all their work up to date could go on the picnic. The teachers always gave fair warning so no kid could claim that he was surprised at the last minute. It was clearly marked on each calendar in the room. More studying and more homework got done the week before the picnic than at any other time of the year.

This year some of the bigger kids hadn't bothered to do all their work. They did not like to carry books home. They wanted to go on the picnic like everybody else, but they were too lazy and too slow to put in the extra effort to get their work done and handed in. They decided to cheat. Since they were bigger than the other kids, they decided to become bullies. They planned to beat up any kids who didn't let them copy their homework.

The other kids didn't like this at all. They formed little gangs. Bullies like to pick on a kid at a time, and not a whole gang of kids. So the kids were able to ignore the bullies, and not help them cheat. The time came for all the homework to be turned in, and none of the bullies had it done. The teacher put their names on the blackboard to let them see that they were not to come to the picnic.

The bullies decided that since they were not permitted to go to the picnic, then nobody would have any fun at the picnic. They planned to make themselves a big nuisance. They planned to put a goldfish and a toad in the punch to make it taste bad. No kid wants to drink fruit juice with a fish swimming in it. And finding a toad in the juice is a good way for a kid to lose his thirst. They also had a lot of firecrackers to set off, the kind that burn slowly and make a big bang and lots of smoke. They also had six rabbits that they planned to let loose, and let a pair of their dogs chase them. Dogs like to chase rabbits, and this can make a big mess if the rabbits are let go by the picnic tables. They planned to continue this mischief until everybody gave up and went home.

The bullies began to act smug. This worried the other students. It was more like the bullies to complain that they were picked on or something like that. The bullies didn't seem to care at all whether or not they could go on the picnic. The good students soon got the feeling that the bullies had something planned, like disrupting the picnic. The kids didn't want the picnic messed up, so they decided to play a little trick on the bullies, just in case. What they did was put a notice on the blackboard that the picnic was postponed until a week later. All the good kids

told each other the true time of the picnic. Only the bullies believed that the picnic was to be a week later.

It worked fine. The picnic was a big success. All the kids and all the teachers had a good time. There were games and prizes and lots of food. The day was warm and sunny. The teachers played the kids in a game of baseball, and the kids won. It seemed that the teachers were a bit too fat to run fast. So, the kids ran faster after the ball, and got to the bases quicker. Even before the nine innings were over, the kids had won the game by a lot of runs, something like sixteen to three. It doesn't take but two or three bad kids to mess up a party or a picnic. This picnic was the best ever, as there wasn't a single bully there.

Maybe the best fun was had the Monday morning after the picnic. All the kids did was talk over all the fun they had had at the picnic. They had cleaned off the blackboard, so there was no proof that a trick had been played on the bullies. There was no clue anywhere stating that the picnic had been postponed.

The bullies were angry. The party was over and done with, and there was no chance at all for messing it up. The bullies had missed the best event of the year, which would not come again until next year. They had to wait until then, and perhaps the good kids would play the same trick on them again. It didn't take long for them to decide that it was not worth it to be a bully. All the fun got missed, and the other kids didn't

like having bullies wanting to play with them.
So, the bullies planned to do their work just like
everybody else, and to stop picking on the smaller
kids. After all, when the picnic comes so seldom,
it is silly to miss it.

THE CHESS CHAMP

Richard was very shy. He did not feel that he was very good at things that most kids did when they were eleven. He did not like to play football, baseball, or basketball. He had no interest in reading the sports pages or reading stories concerning sports people. He kept pretty much to himself. His interest was in the field of math and computers. He planned to be an engineer.

The other kids were crazy over sports. The thing they wanted most was for their team to win at something, to be the best and get a plaque to hang up in the hall of the academy. But no matter who played on their team, they never got their goal. It was frustrating to have no plaque on the wall stating that they had been the best at something, no matter what. They felt that their class needed something to be good in, and most of the boys tried very hard, but to no avail.

One day the principal came into the class and asked if they would get together a chess team. There was to be a city-wide chess contest and he wanted the academy to have an entry. The kids asked Richard to be the captain. He was shy and afraid that he would be a failure. He did not want to take the chance of losing and having the other kids get mad at him or make fun of him. But the kids were certain that he was the smartest kid in class when it came to things like chess, and he had to take the job of captain of the team.

Richard had an older brother, Clarence. Clarence was thirteen, and two classes further on. Clarence had a plan. Since Richard was a whiz at computers, why not use a computer to win the chess matches? They could buy one of those chess computer games where the person plays a game against the computer. Only the best experts in the world could beat a computer. If they used a computer, they were certain to beat all the other kids in the city.

They made up a system. Clarence was to watch the game from some distance. He was to signal the moves to Richard after he put the other kid's move into the computer. It would be exactly like the other kid playing the computer, only he would think he was playing against Richard. Richard did not like the plan, but he was afraid of losing, and having the other kids get mad at him. So he agreed. They made up a code in which each piece of the chessboard had a secret symbol, and each square had a number. They got the system together after only a little practice.

It didn't take long for Richard to beat every other kid in his academy, and move on to the city finals. He felt bad over the fact that he was cheating, but the other kids were so full of praise that he just could not stop. He wanted some other kids to take over, but they would not let him quit. This was the chance for his academy to finally win at something. They wanted that plaque so badly, and Richard was their only hope of getting it.

On the day of the final match, something unexpected happened. While Clarence was on his way to the city park, where the matches were held, his bike hit a hole in the street. He was carrying the chess computer, and it fell off his bike onto the street, and broke. There was neither time nor money to get another. Richard would have to play in the final match with no help. If he was to win, he would have to do it all by himself.

Richard was worried. All the kids from his academy were present, cheering for him. They wanted him to win. They wanted that plaque for their school. His opponent was the son of the math professor at the city college. He had often played chess with his dad, and was very good. He was the best opponent Richard had faced up until this time.

The game did not go nearly as fast as the others in which Richard had played. He had to think for himself, with no help from his computer. He began by trying to think like a computer. He was very careful before making any move, making certain it was the best move, and that there was no trap for him to fall into.

The game took most of the afternoon, but Richard finally got a checkmate and won the game. His classmates cheered wildly. They finally had a plaque for the academy. They were the champs at something. Richard was the most popular kid in all the classes.

Richard felt like confessing that he had used a computer in all the chess games except the last. Clarence talked to him and felt that he should not tell that secret. After all, he won the final game fair and square, against the best kid in the city, who had won all the games against everyone else in the past. Certainly, Richard would have won those other games anyway, as those kids were not nearly as good. He would have beaten them with no computer's help if he had not been so shy. He really hadn't needed that computer. He needed to stop acting so shy and be a friend to other kids.

Richard kept his secret. He stopped his shyness, and never needed to use tricks again. The next year, Richard was the chess champ again, and he did it fair and square, needing no help from any machine.

READING LEVEL FOUR

Difficult Rules Explained
and Made Easy

DIPHTHONGS

There are only four diphthongs in the English language: oi (oy), ei (ey), ou (ow), and ew. Already introduced are the oi as in soil and toil and its alternate spelling oy as in boy and toy, and ei as in weigh, freight, eight, and neighbor and its alternate spelling ey as in they, prey, and whey. In Reading Level Four, the remaining two diphthongs, ou and ew, will be explained.

OU and OW Diphthongs

The ou spelling is usually found in the middle of a word, while the ow spelling usually occurs at the end of the word. The pronunciation is the same with either spelling. In the diphthong ow, the w is being used as a vowel. Letter w can substitute for u because w is really a double u. All diphthongs are a combination of two vowel sounds in which there is a glide from the first vowel sound to the ending sound of the second vowel. The word diphthong means "two utterances". (By contrast, a digraph is two consonant letters that produce an entirely new sound with no change in the mouth position, such as the th in this, that.) Some practice with the ou and ow sounds:

house	mouth	count	down	cow	town
shout	round	bound	bout	how	foul
couch	spout	proud	noun	now	sour
growl	pound	south	found	our	howl
spout	scout	brown	pouch	owl	loud
frown	round	crown	clown	jowl	ouch
cloud	trout	stout	sound	grouch	sour
drown	towel	trout	bound	ground	pout
snout	prowl	sound	flour	crouch	gown

Please note that the diphthong ou sound is different from the ou sound encountered in the words would, should, and could. In these words the ou is pronounced like the short oo sound, as in the words hood and stood. (There are six ways to pronounce the ou sound, which will be taken up later in this level.)

The EW Diphthong

The ew diphthong is pronounced by beginning with the short e sound and ending with the sound of long u. As in the case of the ow diphthong, the w in the ew combination is functioning as the vowel u sound. The ew sound is similar to the ue (long u) sound of blue, true, cue, and hue.

threw	blew	news	new	jew	crew	slew
screw	drew	chew	dew	pew	stew	brew

The AU and AW Combinations

In the previous reading level, it was shown that the consonant letter r can have an effect upon a preceding vowel. The same phenomenon occurs when letter w follows the vowel a. A new sound occurs that is not a diphthong, but a composite, distinctive sound. In the **aw** combination, the w is acting like the <u>consonant</u> letter w, and not as the vowel sound of letter u. This combination is usually spelled **au** in the middle of a word and **aw** at the end of a word. Note that in the **au** spelling the u is acting as a w. Please read the following list with the student to demonstrate this new sound combination.

dawn	maul	jaw	straw	lawn	shawl
yawn	thaw	law	drawn	auto	taunt
flaw	haul	raw	fraud	flaunt	cause
Paul	claw	paw	crawl	launch	fault
bawl	draw	saw	pause	sprawl	haunt

The consonant l, following the letter a, can represent a sound similar to the **aw** sound.

fall	wall	hall	halt	balk	all	chalk
walk	ball	mall	bald	small	call	stall
salt	malt	tall	talk	squall	scald	stalk

To summarize the above: the three consonants that can affect the preceding vowel a to form distinctive vowel-consonant sounds are r, l, and w. It is interesting to note that letters r and l are classified as frictionless consonants called "liquids", and letter w is classified as a semi-vowel.

THE HIATUS

A hiatus is a noteable pause in sound that occurs between two successive vowel sounds in subsequent syllables or words. Because the different vowels are pronounced by utilizing different mouth positions, there must be this lapse in sound while the mouth shifts from one position to the other. When going from one syllable to the next, there is a longer pause between successive vowel sounds than that which occurs between successive consonant sounds or between a vowel and a consonant. Please note the hiatus when the syllable break occurs between vowels:

fluid (flu id)		diet (di et)		riot (ri ot)	
trial	fuel	ruin	neon	video	pliers
giant	poet	trio	duet	radio	create
science	being	minuet	going	stereo	seeing

The hiatus causes confusion for many beginning readers. Problems occur when one must decide whether a two-vowel group is to be pronounced (1) as a long vowel with the second vowel silent, (2) as a diphthong, or (3) as a syllable break, with each vowel pronounced independently. Again, there is no rule. One has to try each way until a recognizable word results. This is not word guessing, but rather a trial of limited possibilities. With practice, pattern recognition assists in doing this automatically. One knows the diphthong combinations, and can readily eliminate them if the pattern is not right, leaving the possibility of either a silent vowel or two pronounced vowels with a hiatus in between. It is the syllable break that determines the final pronunciation. For example, in the word diet in the above list, pronouncing the word with a long i and a silent e makes no sense. Only the successive pronunciations of the i and the e with a hiatus between them gives an understandable word. This is the case with all the words in the above list.

In the French language, great pains are taken to avoid the hiatus. Extra consonants have been inserted in many word constructions to avoid the lapse in sound. Indeed, French is almost unique in having the sound of one word blend with the sound of the next, without a distinct pause. This is the major reason English speakers have difficulty in understanding spoken French, even after they have acquired considerable skill in reading French.

There is a situation in English where the language has been specially constructed to avoid the hiatus. It is in the use of the article an. Before a consonant, the indefinite article is a. Please note:

> a boy   a truck   a car   a girl

Before a vowel, the a is changed to an so that the hiatus of two successive vowels is eliminated. This leads to better understanding.

> an apple   an elephant   an ice cream cone
> an uncle   an old man

SILENT CONSONANTS

The beginning reader is often frustrated when encountering silent letters. A logical question to ask is why they are there in the first place if they have no sound value. The answer is that at one time these letters were indeed pronounced but have had their sound dropped from the pronunciation of the word in accordance with the trend to simplify spoken speech. This is the same reason for the adoption of the schwa. The written word retains these letters so that derivational patterns can be discerned. Fortunately, there are consistencies that can help to identify silent letters in many situations.

The Letter B

When letter b follows the letter m in the same syllable, the b is often silent:

dumb	climb	limb	thumb	comb
bomb	crumb	plumber	numb	lamb

When b is followed by a t in the same syllable, it is often silent: **debt** **doubt**

The Letter D

The letter d is often silent before the ge combination when the preceding vowel is short:

dodge	hedge	ledge	ridge	edge	bridge
judge	budge	pledge	fudge	nudge	budget

Note, however, that there is no d before the ge if there is already a consonant between the vowel and the ge:

revenge	change	hinge	orange	sponge
strange	fringe	binge	plunge	cringe

(The above generalization is useful in spelling. A silent d is inserted before the ge to ensure that the preceding vowel is pronounced short in the case where there is no other consonant before the ge.)

Of course, the letter d may be silent in other situations, such as:

handkerchief   adjective   adjust

The concept to be emphasized is that any letter may become a silent letter in pronouncing a word if that word can still be understood by a listener without that letter being pronounced.

The Letter G

When letter g is followed by an n in the same syllable, the g is usually silent:

| resign | gnat | gnarled | gnu | gnash | gnome |
| assign | sign | consign | gnaw | design | align |

The n in the above words is pronounced slightly differently from the usual n sound. It is the "palatalized n", as in the Spanish word cañon. The g is serving as a diacritic, an indicator of pronunciation. This is retained from the Latin.

The Letter H

Letter h is usually silent when it follows a g at the beginning of a word:

ghost   ghetto   ghastly

Letter h may be unsounded if it is the initial letter in a word:

hour   honor   honest   heir

Letter h of the ch combination may be unsounded if the ch is not a digraph:

| character | stomach | schedule | ache | chorus |
| chemical | chlorine | Christmas | school | anchor |

The GH Combination

The gh combination is frequently silent:

| high | sight | might | slight | fright | light |
| nigh | night | right | flight | blight | tight |

Please note that letter i before the gh combination is pronounced long.

In Early Modern English, there were three ways to pronounce the h sound. The gh sound had been pronounced like the ch sound as in the composer's name Bach, and the g served as a silent indicator of pronunciation. This gh combination became silent in the 17th century.

The silent gh combination frequently follows the vowel combinations of au and ou. In the ou situation, there are six different ways of pronunciation that will be taken up later in this chapter. The following is, at present, for the teacher's information. After the ou combinations are taken up, the student may be referred back to this exercise.

bought	though	although	dough	through
taught	sought	daughter	ought	brought
caught	fought	thorough	nought	borough

When the gh is not silent, it is a digraph with the sound of f, which is explained later in this chapter.

cough   enough   laugh   tough

The Letter K

The letter k is silent when it begins a word and is followed by n:

knack   know   knight   knuckle   knowledge   knot
knock   knob   knife   knell   knapsack   knee

Sometimes the letter k is used to distinguish between homonyms (words that sound alike):

night knight   not knot

The Letter L

The letter l is often silent when it is followed by another consonant in a syllable:

calf   folk   talk   yolk   salmon   half   stalk

The Letter N

The letter n is silent when it follows m in a syllable:

condemn   autumn   solemn

The Letter P

The letter p is often silent when it begins a word and is followed by s:

psychology   psalm   pseudo   psyche   psychosis

P is often silent after m:

pumpkin   empty   prompt   glimpse

Sometimes the p is simply unsounded:

raspberry   cupboard

The Letter S

The letter s is, rarely, silent when it follows an i:

isle   island

The Letter T

The letter t is silent when it follows s and the s is not part of the st digraph:

listen	whistle	fasten	chestnut	moisten
rustle	glisten	hasten	castle	wrestle

An attempt to pronounce the two voiceless consonants s and t in succession is not possible without a hiatus in between. This is awkward in speech, and the t is simply unsounded.

The t is frequently silent before ch. (Some speakers prefer to pronounce it, however, which is equally correct.)

pitch	hatch	match	itch	sketch	batch
watch	patch	ditch	latch	scratch	catch

Please note that a t separates the ch from a <u>short</u> vowel. If another consonant separates the vowel and the ch, there is no t in the spelling:

birch   punch   crunch   drench   pinch

It is evident that the t has been inserted in the spelling pattern tch to ensure that a preceding vowel is pronounced short. This is the same situation as the d being inserted before the ge to get the dge combination as has already been noted. If the ch is preceded by a long vowel, then no t is present before the ch combination:

coach   preach   speech   bleach   touch

The Letter W

The w is silent when it follows letter o and is not a diphthong:

snow	low	bow	hollow	show	row	stow
crow	mow	tow	follow	throw	flow	slow

The w can be silent following an s:

answer   sword

Letter w is often silent when it precedes an r:

wrest	wreck	wriggle	wrist	wry	wrath
wreath	wring	wrestle	wrangle	wrap	write
wrench	wrong	wrinkle	written	writ	wrote

The above is not a complete listing of all the situations in which a letter can be silent, although enough of the common examples of unpronounced letters have been given to illustrate the concept: letters are dropped when it is awkward to pronounce them, or they may be dropped in the interest of speech economy when there is no possibility of resulting misunderstanding.

SILENT VOWELS: SILENT O AND U

Silent U

The vowel u is often silent following a g. This combination is used to preserve the hard g sound.

guide	beguile	morgue	guy	guilty
guess	guardian	fatigue	vague	guitar
plague	disguise	guarantee	guard	guests

There are some words that have a silent u before i:

build   building   built   biscuit

Please note that the u of qu is not always pronounced in the kw manner (quick, quality). Sometimes, in unstressed syllables, the u is silent and the q has the sound of k:

botique   baroque   plaque   mosquito   antique

Silent O

Letter o is often silent in the ou combination:

country   famous   young   cousin   courage
trouble   double   touch   couple   journal

The o is frequently dropped in ous endings:

enormous   hideous   gorgeous   famous   serious
generous   nervous   dangerous fabulous curious

THE OU COMBINATION

This is the most difficult letter combination in English. It can stand for six different sounds. In order to appreciate the manner by which six sounds came to be constructed from only two letters, it is necessary to demonstrate the underlying logic and phonic principles for each of the sounds. The six different sounds of ou are as follows:

1. The diphthong ou. This has already been explained. It is presented here for the sake of completeness.

house   south   mouth   plough

2. The short oo sound. This rule has already been discussed. Here, the second vowel of the ou, the u, serves to combine with the first vowel to give the oo sound.

could   would   should
(This is the sound of oo as in hood and stood.)

3. The long sound of oo. Since the oo sound has both a short and a long pronunciation, as already explained, the ou can produce the long oo sound, too.

you   through   souvenier   tourist   caribou

4. The long o sound of ou. In this case, the u acts in the traditional way of lengthening the first vowel, the o, and remains silent itself.

shoulder   cantaloupe   carousel   dough   poultry
although   camouflage   thorough   though   boulder

5. The short o sound. Here, the u of ou is simply dropped (has become both silent and non-effectual) and the ou has the sound of a short o.

thought   sought   ought   fought   bought   brought

6. The short u sound. In this combination, the o is silent without affecting the u. Thus, the ou combination is pronounced like a short u.

couple	trouble	young	rough
double	country	enough	tough
cousin	southern	famous	touch

The above six ways of pronouncing the ou are important in discerning the approach to pronouncing a new word containing the ou. One has to proceed by trial and error. This is not guessing. With guessing, there is no choice between alternatives. In the ou situation, the student tries each of the <u>phonic</u> possibilities until he arrives at a sound that is a recognizable word.

THE EA COMBINATION

There are three ways to pronounce the ea sound. As in the case of the ou combination, each may have to be tried before one arrives at the sound that forms a recognizable word. These three ways are as follows:

1. The long sound of e. This is the traditional sound, in which the second vowel of a syllable causes the first to lengthen, and the second vowel is then silent.

meat	beat	wheat	cream	fear	seal	rear
each	neat	freak	beach	gear	meal	hear
beak	team	teach	dream	leak	spear	weak
heat	leap	reach	stream	real	peach	deal

2. The short sound of e. Here, the ea combination is pronounced as if the a did not exist.

heard	heaven	instead	dread	dead	ready
sweat	health	leather	thread	lead	tread
bread	wealth	feather	steady	head	meant
death	spread	weather	breath	meadow	heavy

3. The long a sound. In this instance, the ea is like an inverted spelling, and gives the phonic sound of long a as if the combination were spelled ae.

tear   pear   break   great   steak   bear   wear   swear

As in the ou combination, the reader has to try each of the three ea possibilities and that sound which produces a recognizable word is the correct pronunciation.

Before letter r, the ea sound is affected according to whether or not it has a long or a short sound. The long sound is unaffected, but the short ea sound is reduced to the schwa sound by the following letter r.

Schwa sound:

learn   search   pearl   heard   earth   earn

Non-schwa (long sound):

gear   fear   hear   tear   bear

DIGRAPHS (CONCLUDED)

Digraphs are two-consonant combinations in which the resulting sound is unlike that of the letters from which it is formed. In Level One, the digraphs ch, sh, th, wh, and ng were explained. Now the last two English digraphs, the gh and ph, will be discussed.

The PH Digraph

This digraph is pronounced with an f sound. Many words using the ph are of Greek origin, and ph is a Greek spelling for the equivalent f sound in English.

paragraph	asphalt	catastrophe	alphabet
geography	orphan	hemisphere	elephant
telephone	gopher	photograph	symphony
physician	trophy	philosophy	pheasant
sophomore	hyphen	emphasis	pamphlet
autograph	nephew	dolphin	emphatic
physical	phrase	phantom	prophecy

These are unusually difficult words. The point in presenting them is to show that phonic rules are necessary especially when encountering new and unusual words. If the reader does not have these words in his vocabulary, he will not automatically learn them from encountering them in his reading material. The student should be getting to the point that he can be taught to look up new words in the dictionary, and note the dictionary methods of indicating pronunciation.

The GH Digraph

When the gh combination is not silent, it is a digraph with the sound of f. This pronunciation survived from a dialect of English, and is found in relatively few words.

tough   rough   cough   enough   laugh   laughter

HOW MANY SYLLABLES?

It is common, in everyday speech, to drop vowels. This is done whenever there is a desire to communicate more quickly and there is little possibility of being misunderstood. In the following list, please note that if the underlined vowel is dropped, the word is then pronounced with just two syllables instead of three. Many of the vowels are either non-sounds when dropped or schwa sounds when retained. The choice of degree of sounding the underlined vowels resides with the speaker.

marvelous	luxury	ivory	aspirin
desperate	nursery	boundary	funeral
prosperous	decimal	corporal	scenery

More practice words. The underlined vowel may be sounded or go unsounded at the speaker's option. The number of syllables in the word changes accordingly.

general	grocery	bravery	opera	numeral
jewelry	mineral	sophomore	camera	average
diamond	interest	chocolate	violet	history
battery	generous	laboratory	memory	natural
century	favorite	temperature	mystery	factory

While some vowel sounds may be dropped from speech, they may never be dropped from written English. Ignorance of this fact is another reason for poor spelling.

HOW MANY SYLLABLES? (CONTINUED)

It is necessary to have a vowel for every syllable or, by definition, there cannot be a syllable. Some syllables are quite long and have only one pronounced vowel. This leads to confusion and an attempt to create additional syllables where they cannot exist due to the absence of vowels. Some one-syllable words:

drowned	crowned	blessed	tipped	jerked
stuffed	crammed	flipped	trapped	maimed
clogged	slammed	planned	shrugged	jammed

This special **ed** ending was explained in Level Two, as the case in which the **ed** ending is tacked on and not pronounced as a separate syllable.

Some two-syllable words that resemble three-syllable words:

monstrous (mon strous)   hindrance (hin drance)
attacked (at tacked)   lightning (light ning)
necklace (neck lace)   wondrous (won drous)
burglar (bur glar)   laundry (laun dry)
hungry (hun gry)   athlete (ath lete)

In the above list, proper division into syllables makes it evident that these are two- and not three-syllable words.

Some three syllable words:

    mischievous (mis chie vous)
    performance (per form ance)
    disastrous (dis as trous)
    providence (prov i dence)
    barbarous (bar ba rous)

The point of the above is that proper syllable division is necessary for proper pronunciation. In encountering new long words, use of a dictionary is advised. Indeed, from now on, dictionary usage can be of help in both syllable division and pronunciation in addition to providing meanings.

COMPOUND WORDS

One of the most consistent rules in both spelling and phonics concerns the formation of compound words. The rule is to <u>use</u> <u>all</u> <u>the</u> <u>letters</u> <u>in</u> <u>the</u> <u>smaller</u> <u>words</u> <u>in</u> <u>making</u> <u>up</u> <u>the</u> <u>compound</u> <u>word</u>. The syllable break occurs between the smaller words and they are pronounced as individual words that have been joined. That is, they have a shorter pause in sound between the syllables as a joined (compound) word than they would if they were separate words pronounced in succession. There is generally a short pause between syllables, a longer pause between words, and a still longer pause between sentences. Of course, the longest pause comes between paragraphs.

Some common compound words. Note that all the letters of the smaller words are retained:

blueprint	applesauce	extraordinary	giveaway
safeguard	thereafter	nevertheless	sidewalk
blueberry	typewriter	wastebasket	nowadays
whereupon	sidetrack	whereabouts	farewell
pineapple	wholesale	moreover	homework

This rule of keeping all the letters of the smaller words in compound words applies even when it results in a doubled consonant where the words join:

overreach	granddaughter	beachhead	teammate
newsstand	knickknack	jackknife	overripe
hitchhike	bookkeeper	cattail	glowworm
bathhouse	withhold	earring	overrule
nighttime	fishhook	overrun	roommate

The above words may look somewhat peculiar, especially the double h in fishhook, but they are correct English spellings.

MISCELLANEOUS

The word one is unphonic. It is pronounced as if spelled wun. It was once phonic, and has now kept the prior sound value while undergoing spelling changes. One is derived from the Indo-European word oi-nos (like the Latin-derived word unit). The oi is a diphthong containing the w sound. The word oi-nos was shortened in Middle English to oon, and finally to the modern one.

Many words that are now unphonic have undergone similar changes. Sometimes, though, it has been poor spelling that somehow got started and is now entrenched. A good example of this is found in the ceed, cede, and sede endings. Proceed is spelled differently from precede, although they both derive from the exact same Latin root, cedere, (go, withdraw, or yield). Please note the different endings of succeed, concede, and supersede. It is helpful to note that the cede spelling for this sound is used in all words except succeed, proceed, exceed, and supersede.

Another incomplete spelling change is the substitution of y for i. Letter y was introduced into Latin at the time of the Republic to facilitate the spelling of words of Greek origin. The y spelling of words like mayor, crayon, and canyon gives the syllable a feeling of stopping, of a yuh sound. The i spelling in words like union and spaniel lacks this needed yuh sound. How much more convenient it would be for the beginning reader if the following words were spelled with a y instead of an i:

Daniel	behavior	union	billion
junior	rebellion	onion	bullion
senior	companion	spaniel	opinion

The ion sounded as yon goes back to the Latin, where an i before another vowel was pronounced as the consonant sound of y.

SUMMARY OF PHONIC RULES
READING LEVEL FOUR

1.   The diphthong ou and its alternate spelling ow are found in words like:

       house, cow, shout, and growl.

The ew diphthong has the sound of long u. It is found in words like:

       stew, news, screw, and brew.

2.   The combination au (and its alternate spelling aw) is not a diphthong. It has a unique sound. Examples:

       dawn, haul, pause, and thaw.

3.   Letter l following letter a gives a sound that resembles the aw sound:

       fall, salt, stalk, bald, call.

4.   A hiatus is a slight pause in sound between the pronunciation of two successive vowel sounds.

       diet riot trial create fuel video giant

5.   Silent consonants are letters that remain in words but are not pronounced. They had sound value at one time, but no longer retain it. Some examples are the b of dumb, the d in hedge, the g in sign, the h of ghost, the gh of sight, the k of knife, the l of half, the n of autumn, the p of pseudo, the s of island, the t of listen, and the w of low.

6.   Silent vowels occur along the same principles as silent consonants.

The vowel u is often silent following a g, as in:

       guide, guilty, guard, and guess.

The vowel o is often silent in the ou combination, as in the words:

       famous, double, cousin, and touch.

7. The ou combination has six ways of being pronounced:
   a. As the diphthong: house, south, mouth
   b. As a short oo sound: could, would, should
   c. As a long oo sound: you, through, caribou
   d. As a short o sound: ought, cough, fought, bought
   e. As a long o sound: dough, though, shoulder
   f. As a short u sound: rough, enough, trouble, country
8. The ea combination is pronounced in three ways:
   a. The long sound of e: meat, cream, team, teach
   b. The short e sound: dead, heaven, thread, breath
   c. The long a sound: break, steak, great, pear
9. Digraphs are concluded in this level with the addition
of two new ones:

   The **ph** digraph is pronounced as an f: phrase, hyphen,
asphalt, orphan.

   The **gh** digraph is pronounced as an f: tough, rough,
laugh, cough.
10. Some words drop a syllable, usually a vowel, in
ordinary speech. Please note that the following may be
pronounced with either two or three syllables:

   iv_o_ry lux_u_ry fun_e_ral corp_o_ral dec_i_mal
11. Compound words retain all their letters when they join
to form one word:

   overripe roommate newsstand
   fishhook nowadays nevertheless
12. Some words are spelled with an i where a y would be
preferable because of the y_uh_ sound of y:

   billion junior union onion

LEVEL FOUR STORIES

1. THE LOCKSMITH

2. THE PAPER ROUTE

3. THE SHOW HORSE

4. THE RESTAURANT

These stories contain words that have phonic aspects explained in Levels One, Two, Three, and Four. If the student has any difficulties, please refer back to the appropriate exercises.

THE LOCKSMITH

Daniel's dad had a locksmith shop. It was full of things like locks, keys, and safes. Daniel was eleven years old, and all his friends called him by his nick-name, Danny. He had already decided to be a locksmith when he grew up. His dad gave him lots of jobs to do around the shop. Danny liked to make keys in the duplicating machine for the customers. He particularly liked to change the key to a lock. This was necessary whenever people moved into a new home and were not certain if strangers had keys to their new house. It was not necessary to change the entire lock. All that was needed was to take out the lock's cylinder and insert different pins. Then, a new key was made that could turn the cylinder and the old key did not work any more.

There was one thing that Danny kept secret. It was that he knew how to pick locks. It is important for locksmiths to open locks when there is no key. People are frequently locking themselves out of their cars and offices and houses. If these locks had to be drilled open, they would be ruined, and a new lock would be needed. A good locksmith picks the lock and then takes the lock apart so that a new key can be made. Whenever there were no customers around, Danny opened the locks that had no keys. He was

even better at it than his dad. Danny had a
better feel for when the picking tools were doing
the job right. He knew when the pins were aligned
in the cylinder and he knew how much torque to use
with the little tweezer-like tool that was
inserted into the keyslot. Danny knew so much
about locksmithing that he got the hardest locks
to pick that came into the shop. He also had the
toughest keys to duplicate, because nobody ever
had to jiggle a key in a lock when Danny had made
it. His keys always fit perfectly.

One day something happened at school. A
parent came to see the teacher about her child and
brought the youngest child along. That child was
only three years old, and began wandering around
the school. The mother and the teacher did not
notice that child was gone until they heard some
screaming. Little Johnny had gone into the
utility closet and slammed the door shut and
couldn't get out. The teacher tried to open the
door but it had locked automatically when it shut.
Johnny began to scream louder and to bang things
in that dark closet. The principal came but she
couldn't find the proper key for the lock on the
door. Neither could the janitor. Johnny began
pushing on the bottles that were on the shelves
and some fell to the floor and broke. The mother
began screaming, too, as she was afraid that
Johnny was going to get cut on that glass. Soon
there was a big crowd of kids in the hall around
the closet door. The teacher told the janitor to
call the police and the fire department.

Danny went to the teacher and told her that he would get the door open if she would send all the kids back to their classrooms. She knew that Danny's dad had a locksmith shop and that Danny liked locks, but she didn't see what Danny could do. Danny whispered into her ear that he knew how to pick that lock and that he did not want the other kids to see how it was done. The teacher got the principal to make all the kids go back to their classrooms. The mother became calm when she saw Danny get to work on the lock. Danny had a few of his tools with him. He put his locksmith tweezers into the slot and applied a twisting force. Then he inserted one of his small picks into the key slot. He jiggled and felt and in a moment the door was open. The principal was so surprised that she could hardly believe her eyes. The mother picked up little Johnny and was relieved to see that he was not hurt. The janitor wanted to know just what Danny had done to get that door open so fast.

Danny did not want any publicity. He told the teacher that locksmith tools are sometimes used by burglars to open locks. Therefore, it is against the law to have them if you are not a bonded locksmith. He just happened to have some tools in his pocket that he forgot to put on his workbench when he left his dad's shop. It would probably get him into trouble if she told anyone what he did. He was just glad that he had learned something that enabled him to help someone else.

The principal did phone Danny's dad to tell him what Danny had done and how pleased they were

that he had helped out in that emergency. This
made his dad very happy. Danny's dad knew that
Danny would be one of the very best locksmiths
when he grew up. Good locksmiths never show off
their tricks. If the wrong people learned how to
pick locks, lots of things would no longer be
protected. Danny was not only a good locksmith,
he was also a smart boy.

THE PAPER ROUTE

Joseph had a paper route so that he could earn some extra spending money. His dad gave him an allowance every Friday, but it never lasted beyond Tuesday or Wednesday, and he hated being broke toward the end of the week. There were always those extra things that he wanted to do, like go to the movies or play the video games at the shopping center, and he didn't like it when his parents asked him why he wanted extra money or wanted to borrow against next week's allowance.

His town had two newspapers, a morning and an afternoon paper. He had chosen to deliver the afternoon paper after school. He did not like the idea of getting out of a warm bed early on cold winter mornings to deliver papers before going to school.

Because his pay was just three cents for each paper delivered, he decided to take on two routes at the same time. He called it a double route because he had twice as many papers to deliver and could make twice as much money. The average route had fifty customers. With his double route, he had a hundred customers. His earnings were three dollars a day, enough to buy all the little extras and to provide enough money to play Pac Man and other video games so that he could get the best scores and be the video game champion player of all the kids in his neighborhood. The problem was that it could take so much time to deliver the newspapers that there wouldn't be time to go to the shopping center and play the video machines before he had to go home for supper. It was necessary to find ways to hustle in order to fit all his activities into so little time.

He drew up a map of his route area. To save time, he did not want to back-track or go over the same street twice. He found short cuts by going through narrow alleyways. He looked for places where he could cut across lawns and vacant ground. He knew all the spots in the hedges along the way that were large enough for him to get through with his bike and sack of papers. He even used a hammer to loosen boards in fences in certain areas so that he might create a shortcut where one had not heretofore existed. He sought to save as much distance as possible in order to get in some time with the video games before it was time to go home for supper each evening.

He had his dad build some wire baskets that attached to his bike in such a way that he could now carry more papers than before. He didn't like to use a sack that had a strap over his shoulder because that did not allow his arms to be free enough to throw the papers as accurately as he needed to do. Customers like to get their papers on their doorsteps and not on the lawn where they can get wet in case of rain. He had learned that happy customers tend to give bigger tips, and bigger tips mean more money to put into the video game machines.

What took the most time was collecting the money from the customers. This was done on Fridays. While most of the people had the money ready for him, some people were almost never at home when he had the opportunity to collect. This meant that he had to return over and over again to a few houses which took up a lot of time. He got the idea of having a small money box at those people's houses. He drew up a plan for such a box and took it to his friend Daniel. It was a simple thing to make. It was a small box with a slot cut in the top. The front of the box consisted of a door with a lock on it. The customer was supposed to put the money in the box so that all Joseph had to do on Friday was open the box with his key and take out the money. The box was fastened to a wooden post or board with some screws that were tightened from the inside. You had to have the box open to fasten or loosen the screws. This was so that nobody could steal the box by simply unscrewing the screws and taking it. Danny made six of these boxes for Joseph, all opening with the same key. Now Joseph would not have to keep returning to the same houses to collect, as the money would be waiting for him. Daniel charged only a dollar for each box, because Joseph was a good friend and he wanted to help him out.

Joseph also had a locked money box on his bicycle. The box had a timer on it so that it could not be opened until eight in the evening. This was to discourage anyone from trying to steal his money from him after he had collected it.

The manager of the newspaper was having trouble getting enough kids to deliver the papers. There wasn't enough profit to make it worthwhile for the average kid. The manager noted that Joseph did not seem to have any trouble delivering a double route, and asked if he could go along sometime and see for himself how it was done. He went with Joseph and was very impressed. The manager decided to create a new job called the Manager of Newspaper Delivery. He offered it to Joseph. The purpose of the job was to teach kids how to deliver papers quickly. Whenever there was a turnover, there was a problem. A turnover is when someone quits and another takes over. Joseph's new job was to teach the new kid the tricks needed to get the papers delivered easily and quickly. Joseph's new job paid a lot more than he earned doing his own deliveries, and he was pleased to turn over his routes to another kid.

The two things that helped make Joseph's program a success were the newspaper racks for the bicycles and the customer's money boxes for those people who were hard to collect from. The newspaper bought the racks for the delivery boys, but they had to give them back or turn them over to their successor if they quit the delivery job.

Joseph had the idea of giving girls a chance at being newspaper delivery persons. It doesn't sound right to call a girl a paperboy when she has a paper route. It also doesn't sound right to call her a papergirl. So Joseph called all the kids who delivered newspapers paperkids. It didn't sound right at first, but soon everyone got used to the name.

Soon Joseph had everything going so well that all he had to do was ride around the town on his bicycle and watch for problems the paperkids might be having in delivering the papers. If he saw any problems, he helped the kids solve them. The customers were pleased to be getting their papers quicker, and soon the newspaper was selling more papers. This made the manager very happy. He told Joseph that he would consider hiring him as a reporter when he grew up. Joseph's dad was very proud of him, and told him that the best way for a person to get ahead in this world was to think up ways of getting more done in less time. This was exactly what Joseph had done. But, best of all, Joseph had enough money to buy video games that he could play at home. He found that better than hanging around the video arcades and pumping quarters into the machines. Now he could have his fun and keep his money, the best thing any kid could want.

THE SHOW HORSE

Catherine and Diane were best friends. They lived in adjacent houses next to one another in a rural neighborhood. What both girls enjoyed most was hiking in the mountains near their homes. Diane liked to draw and would often sketch the houses in the town below. Catherine would sit on a tree limb and watch, amazed that a piece of blank paper could become so pretty with only a few strokes of a pencil. It was autumn and the scenery was magnificent when the leaves began to turn into the fall colors of red, yellow, orange, and even purple.

It was on a Tuesday morning when they found a horse on the mountain trail. He was a big stallion and apparently quite used to people. He let the girls approach and pet him without seeming to be nervous. It was Cathy's guess that he was a famous show horse. Diane thought that maybe he was a race horse but he somehow seemed too gentle for that. His tail and mane had some briars stuck in them. He had probably spent the night in the woods.

Cathy had taken a few riding lessons the year before, when her family had taken a trip to a dude ranch. She got on the horse's back. He didn't object. Diane then got on, too, and they indicated the way he was to take them. The horse

understood and went back down the trail. It was wonderful fun to be on a horse's back and go through the woods. It would be wonderful to keep this horse and do this over and over again.

The girls made up a plan. They intended to disguise the horse so that it looked like just any old regular horse. They took the horse to an old barn on a neighbor's property that had been unused for a long time. They found some old horse blankets that had moth holes in them. It made the horse look like an old nag from a distance. They purposely combed his mane improperly to enhance the look of shabbiness. Then they rubbed dirt on his shiny hooves and put some mud on his shiny coat. He now looked like a pauper, whereas before he had looked like a prince. They decided to call him Prince.

The girls found some old riding gear in the neighbor's barn. It was an English saddle and western reins. To somebody who knew about horses, it was an awful sight. They knew that, and felt it seemed to enhance the disguise. They took turns riding Prince, and were pleased that he obeyed so well.

But there was a major problem. It was food for Prince. There was plenty of grass around, but the girls knew that this horse had been given a very good diet. Otherwise his coat would not be so shiny and he would not look so healthy. The horses that were left in a field all day to graze on weeds and grass didn't have such an alert manner, nor did they have as much energy and spirit. So the girls went to the feed store to buy some alfalfa hay and some grain. They were astonished at the prices. Hay cost over four dollars a bale and the grain was six dollars for a fifty pound sack. They saw signs on the wall advertising services for horses. Horseshoeing was twenty-five dollars. The services of a veterinarian ranged from twenty to fifty dollars for a routine visit. Saddles and other paraphernalia like horse spray and lead ropes and bridles were much higher in price than they had ever imagined.

The girls realized that it was just a dream that they could keep Prince for their very own. They got the man to give them half a sack of grain for three dollars. He let them rake up some alfalfa from the storage area, pieces that had fallen loose from the bales that were neatly stacked all the way up to the roof. This they put in a wagon to pull home.

As they were leaving they saw a poster on the wall. It had a photograph of Prince on it. The poster promised a reward for anybody finding the horse. It gave a telephone number. The owner of the feed store said that Prince was a famous Arabian show horse and had won many blue ribbons. He was worth many thousands of dollars.

The girls hurried home. They were very excited. Now they knew that it was impossible for them to keep Prince, and they were wondering what kind of a reward was offered for his return. They took the hay and grain to Prince and then told their parents that they had found a valuable horse. The owner was relieved to get their telephone call and said that he'd be over to their place just as soon as he could get finished with some important business he was doing.

But Prince was hardly a magnificent Arabian show horse the way they had disguised him. They didn't want the owner to get mad, so they decided to change him back from a pauper look into a prince look. They got brushes and a horse comb from the feed store, along with hoof polish. They combed and brushed and polished and in a little while the horse looked just as splendid as he looked in that photograph on the reward poster.

The owner was delighted to find the horse in such good shape. He had worried that there might be some injuries, or that his mane or tail might be damaged. But the horse was in perfect shape, ready for the big horse show in a few days. The horse had gotten loose from a corral a few miles away when somebody had forgotten to secure the gate properly.

Cathy's and Diane's parents were impressed with the love the girls had shown for that horse. The owner suggested that the girls have horses for their reward. He had some older horses that no longer had the spunk to compete in horse shows but were nevertheless still excellent riding horses. He would give each girl a horse, complete with riding gear and all the paraphernalia needed for complete care. Also, he would supply all the feed for the horses for a whole year. The girls were pleased when their parents said that they could accept the horses. It was like a dream come true.

Now the girls enjoyed going to the woods even more. Instead of walking, they rode. Somehow, even the best view becomes better from the back of a horse.

THE RESTAURANT

Andrew and his friend Pamela had working mothers. That means that they had no one to stay at home with them, because both mom and dad did not get home from their jobs until after five o'clock. The kids were neighbors and during the summer they often played together the entire day. Each of their mothers would make a lunch for them before she left for the day. They were supposed to keep out of trouble and stay near home until mom got home to prepare supper.

The two kids got to eat lunch together. They would take their lunches onto the porch and set up a table and pretend they had an outdoor restaurant. They had seen photographs of such restaurants in travel books, most often in places like France and Italy. They really didn't like the cold lunches left by their mothers, and started cooking for each other. It started quite simply. Andrew would pretend his place was a famous restaurant, and he would take Pam's order. He would cook whatever she wanted and serve it, making enough for the two of them. Then, the next day she would pretend that she had a restaurant and be the cook and waitress and serve him. It was great fun.

Soon some other kids saw what they were doing and joined in on the fun. At first they just let the other kids eat free. But then they got the idea of starting a kids' restaurant. There were plenty of children who had working parents and were left home to fend for themselves for the entire day. They didn't like cold sandwiches and cold sodas.

It started out small and grew to the point that Andrew and Pam were serving as many as twenty kids for lunch. Andrew was the cook most of the time, and Pamela was the waitress. They didn't charge much. A bowl of onion soup cost ten cents. Bread cost five cents for two slices. A sandwich with slices of meat and cheese cost fifteen cents. For dessert there was a choice of ice cream or cake or pudding or whatever they could find in their mothers' kitchens.

It was nice for Pamela that her mother kept a well stocked larder. On some days she was able to serve chestnut soup. Spaghetti was a favorite, with meat sauce. On some days Pam made a large salad, with lettuce, tomatoes, sliced onions, celery, cucumbers, carrots, and whatever else she could find in the kitchen. She put a thick mayonnaise dressing on the salad. For drinks she had chocolate milk, soda, or fruit juice.

The kids did not tell their parents about the restaurant. It was so much fun and mom might object and make them stop. But the parents began to notice the food supplies going down quicker than they had before. They noticed that the dishwasher powder was almost all gone. And they

noticed little chips and scratches appearing on their dishes quicker than had ever happened before. They were curious as to why, but did not suspect the real reason.

It was on a Friday when Pam's mom had forgotten to bring some important papers to her office and had to go back home to get them. She decided to do it over her lunch hour. When she pulled her automobile into the driveway of her house, she was astonished to see such a large number of children on her front lawn. She saw her daughter Pam in a waitress dress, serving lunch. She could hardly believe her own eyes. There was a sign stating that this was the Castle Restaurant, serving lunch only, just on weekdays.

She decided to stay in her car a moment and just watch and listen. It was a good group of children, enjoying each other's company just as adults do in similar circumstances. They were getting into no trouble. In fact, she had never seen such a large group of children behave so well.

When Andrew and Pam saw Pam's mother, they got very scared. But she was not at all like they imagined she would be if she found out what they were up to all day while she was away at work. They had thought that she would yell at them and all their friends and customers. But she was very polite and seemed interested in what they were serving and how much it cost on the menu. She even sat down and ordered from the menu. She wanted creamed cheese and olives on crackers, and a bowl of vegetable soup. Pam gave her the best

service. For dessert, she had banana cream pie
and a cup of instant coffee. Her bill was fifty-
five cents. She paid it and left a twenty cent
tip for Pam. She had to hurry back to the office
and left as soon as she was finished. Because it
was Friday, she had a lot of work to finish at the
office before the weekend.

When she got home that night, the lawn was
immaculate. There was no trash anywhere. The
dishes had been washed in the dishwasher and put
away in the proper places. She had noted that her
larder was less full than the last time she had
looked. But she didn't say anything to Pam at
all, which puzzled her.

The next day, Saturday, Pam's parents invited
Pam and Andrew to go out with them to get lunch at
a restaurant. On the way there they stopped off
at the supermarket to pick up a few things. Pam's
mother remarked about the price of food as she
bought olives, cream cheese, banana cream pie,
sliced meat, sliced cheese, and other things that
had been on the menu of the Castle Restaurant.
The kids were astonished at what those things
cost. She also bought powdered soap for the
dishwasher which was much more expensive than the
kids had thought it was. Mom also bought a few
dishes, and the kids got an idea of what the cups
and saucers and plates that they chipped and
scratched cost to replace. Still, the parents
didn't say anything about the kids' restaurant.

They had lunch at a regular restaurant. When
the kids got to noticing the prices, they realized
how cheap their own prices were. They were the

best bargain in town. There was no way a mother could begin to buy food for the prices they were charging, or even take the time and energy to prepare and serve it. The kids were having fun, but doing a lot of work and making their parents pay the bill.

After lunch, the kids told about their restaurant and why they started it. They were tired of the same food all the time that was left on the table for them to eat by themselves. They now realized that they were feeding all the neighborhood kids almost for free, the way things really cost. They were sorry about that.

Pam's parents talked things over with Andrew's parents and then they went around to the other parents in the neighborhood who had children home alone for the entire day. The parents decided to organize a club and hire someone to make meals for the children. They found a few grandmothers with nothing to do who volunteered to cook the lunches and keep an eye on things. Each parent would pay the real cost of the meals, plus a little extra for the ladies who made and served the meals. There was also a breakage fund to get things replaced if need be.

Things worked out very well for Pamela and Andrew. They were getting tired of doing all the work every day. They felt that they were too young to have such a commitment and were glad to be out of the restaurant business. But it was certainly a worthwhile experience. The best was that now they had a place to meet the gang and be part of the gang, not just the cook and waitress.

READING LEVEL FIVE

Regular Irregularities –
Spelling and Phonic Rules Made Easy

CONSONANT SOUND CHANGE BEFORE LETTER U

It has been noted that certain consonants can affect the pronunciation of preceding vowels. In Reading Level Three it was shown that letter r can change the pronunciation of the preceding short vowel, as in words like car, bird, burst, perch, and lord. In Reading Level Four it was shown that the consonants w and l have an effect on the pronunciation of the preceding vowel a, as in words like dawn, claw, yawn, salt, and stalk. This is due to the frictionless consonant quality of letters r and l, and to the semi-vowel quality of letter w.

In Reading Level Five an opposite situation will be discussed, which is the case of consonants being affected by succeeding vowels. Words with such letter combinations are among the most difficult to pronounce and spell in the English language.

THE TU AND DU COMBINATIONS

When the consonant d or t precedes the letter u in the same syllable, the resulting sound can be like the sound of the ch digraph in the word choo-choo. Please have the student read the following list, keeping this in mind.

future	mutual	nature	gesture
culture	creature	mature	fixture
capture	graduate	signature	feature
lecture	schedule	adventure	educate
picture	fracture	sculpture	situate
gradual	punctual	furniture	mixture
pasture	victuals	fortunate	vulture
eventual	procedure	individual	statute

However, it should be noted that the t or d does not affect the u in this way at the beginning of a word. The effect occurs only in the latter syllable or syllables. Some examples of the unaffected u at the beginning of words:

duck   dunce   duke   tube   tuck   tumble

The reason for changing the pronunciation of the letter u in the later syllables goes back to the observation that the d and t sounds are made by stopping and releasing the air stream (Level One). It is awkward to go from the _final_ sound of the d or t into the lip position needed for pronouncing the vowel u. In rapid speech this d or t takes on the ch sound for euphony, because it is easier to pronounce the u after a ch sound than after sounding a final letter d or t. Pronouncing a d or t with a ch sound avoids

an artificial syllable break when the du and tu are
encountered in the latter part of a word. Re-reading the
list above with this in mind should make this concept clear.
The point is that letters are often given different sound
values, depending on preceding and succeeding letters, in
the interest of euphony and to avoid unnecessary gaps in
sound when pronouncing a word.

THE TI, SI, AND CI COMBINATIONS

When the letter i is preceded in a syllable by the
consonants t, s, or c, forming the ti, si, and ci
combinations, and this combination is followed by a vowel,
the sound is like the digraph sh in the word she. Note the
pronunciation of the words mention, pension, and facial.
They all contain the sh sound. Please read the following
words with the student and note this sh sound:

composition	ambition	action	nation
information	vacation	situation	initial
substantial	position	intention	martial
construction	patience	operation	partial
satisfaction	condition	correction	tuition
conversation	completion	collection	caution
confidential	reflection	occupation	portion

gracious	special	delicious	especially
precious	suspicion	efficient	politician
official	sufficient	financial	commercial

impression	recession	expression	succession
permission	admission	progression	compassion
commission	possession	intermission	confession

It may seem odd that such diverse spellings as ci, si, and ti give the same **sh** sound, but there is a reason for this. It has already been noted that c before i is always pronounced s, and therefore the ci and si sounds are the same sound with different spellings. The s and t are both unvoiced consonants and need a following vowel to carry their sound. Thus, the ti and si are virtually equivalent in unstressed syllables. The rule states that <u>the</u> <u>sh</u> <u>sound</u> <u>does</u> <u>not</u> <u>occur</u> <u>unless</u> <u>the</u> <u>ci,</u> <u>si,</u> <u>or</u> <u>ti</u> <u>is</u> <u>followed</u> <u>by</u> <u>a</u> <u>vowel</u>. This following of letter i by another vowel in the same syllable would ordinarily require the i to be pronounced long, or the two vowels would have to be split into separate syllables with a hiatus in between as in the pronunciation of <u>riot</u> and <u>radio.</u>

The sh sound of ci, si, and ti that results when these combinations are before a vowel in the same syllable is, in the interest of speech economy, to avoid creating another syllable: the sh sound blends easily with the following vowel. In the absence of some explanation to the reader, as given above, there is a tendency to spell words like nation with a "shun", giving "nashun", as any teacher has experienced. Rather than tell the student that there is no reason for the "shun" sound of nation, and frustrate him into thinking that he has to deal with an illogical language that has to be accepted and memorized by rote, point out the rule. A student will soon enough encounter plenty of words that have this sh sound, and the response will become automatic.

Unfortunately, rules in phonics are rarely free of exceptions. Concerning the rule that the **tion** spelling is pronounced **shun,** there is such an exception. Please note the following words:

combustion   congestion   digestion   exhaustion
suggestion   question   celestial

In the above words, the ti does not have the sh sound, but takes instead the ch sound. This is because of the s that precedes the ti. It is awkward to pronounce an sh (ti) sound after an s, so the sh is pronounced as if it were a ch. As explained before, this change in sound is in the interest of euphony and serves to avoid a sound gap between the syllables.

There is a special situation concerning the sion ending when the s is preceded by a sounded vowel. It was noted in Level One that the letter s takes on a z sound whenever it follows an accentuated vowel or voiced consonant. This is because s is the unvoiced counterpart of z. S is the sound that results from pronunciation without involvement of the vocal cords, while z is a voiced counterpart. Thus, in the list below, the sh phoneme changes to the zh phoneme.

decision   provision   erosion   confusion
revision   television   delusion   explosion
occasion   conclusion   illusion   collision

THE SH SOUND OF SUGAR

In some common words, letter s before u is pronounced like an sh. Please note the following examples:

sugar   sure   insurance   issue   pressure

The above words are exceptions to the general rule, which is that an s before a u is simply pronounced s, as in the following words:

subject　ʹsuspense　　suck　suffer　Sunday　suppose

It is possible that because of a look-alike similarity with words containing du and tu that have the ch sound, the su sound became associated with the sh sound for some words. This could have occured in a dialect, and then spread into the general language. A famous example of mispronunciation occured in the Spanish court of Philip II. The king had a lisp, and the courtiers began imitating his methods of pronunciation, resulting in the modern Castilian manner of pronunciation. Such a situation of mispronunciation possibly also occured with the English words sugar, sure, etc.

THE ZH SOUND OF TREASURE

Please note the zh phoneme in the following words:

measure	Asia	usual	treasure
leisure	casual	casualty	pleasure

In these words, the s is acting to form the digraph sound of sh, but the vibrating vocal cords of the preceding accentuated vowel sound change the s to a z, thus changing the sh to a zh sound. This occurs naturally when speaking, and is mentioned here to illustrate that many pronunciations are simply the result of a tendency to economize in making sounds. It is interesting to note that the zh phoneme came into use in the 17th century, providing a voiced partner for the unvoiced sh.

THE PREFIX

A prefix is a syllable added to the beginning of a word to alter its meaning. One of the most consistent rules governing its addition is that <u>when the prefix ends with the same letter that begins the word that it joins, both letters are retained in the spelling of the resulting word.</u> Please note:

dissent	reelection	unnail	reerect
reelect	dissatisfy	reedit	unnamed
reenact	unnurtured	misstep	unnoted
reenter	cooperation	missent	misspent
dissect	reemphasize	dissenter	reemerge
dissever	reestablish	dissocial	dissolve
dissuade	dissymmetry	dissemble	reeducate
reenlist	unnecessary	unnoticed	cooperate
misspell	unnavigated	reexamine	dissonant
unneeded	unnegotiable	unnameable	dissatisfy
misstate	misstatement	dissonance	dissimilar
misshape	unneighborly	disservice	coordinate

Some words without double letters, with the same prefixes:

disappoint	recover	mistrust	rejoin
unimportant	coexist	disappear	regain
disputation	disaster	unopposed	unkind
misunderstood	co-author	unfriendly	unlock
misinformation	co-editor	reconsider	unload

Please note that words beginning with a prefix always

divide into a syllable after the prefix:

un tie   re wind   dis own

(and all the words in the preceding lists.)

THE SUFFIX

A suffix is a syllable added to the end of a word. This syllable can change the meaning of the word or give it a different grammatical function. For example, adding ly can change a noun into an adverb: principal + ly = principally.

The same rule regarding double letters using prefixes applies to suffixes. Note in the list below that when the word ends with the same letter which begins the suffix, both letters are retained in the new word.

truthfully	cruelly	thinness	brownness
principally	finally	meanness	naturally
incidentally	usually	gradually	recoilless
accidentally	actually	eventually	skillfully
successfully	keenness	continually	suddenness

When a word ends with a silent e, the e is retained when adding a suffix beginning with a consonant:

completely	likely	definitely
absolutely	lately	excitement
improvement	scarcely	requirement
commencement	severely	involvement
announcement	extremely	arrangement
encouragement	immensely	immediately
advertisement	sincerely	achievement

However, there are sixteen common words that are exceptions to this rule. Please note:

probably	horribly	doubly	truly
abridgment	possibly	wisdom	ninth
incredibly	judgment	wholly	width
acknowledgment	terribly	argument	awful

It can be instructive to examine the reasons why these words are exceptions. In the case of the words incredibly, horribly, terribly, probably, possibly, and doubly, please note the construction of the adverbial forms:

double   + ly = doublely   but is spelled doubly
possible   + ly = possiblely   but is spelled possibly
probable   + ly = probablely   but is spelled probably
terrible   + ly = terriblely   but is spelled terribly
horrible   + ly = horriblely   but is spelled horribly
incredible + ly = incrediblely   but is spelled incredibly

In the above, the final e and the preceding l are dropped because they are not needed for communicating the meaning of the word. It would be awkward to pronounce a word like horriblely, and it is simplified to the common (now correct) spelling, horribly.

In the case of **wide + th**, if it were spelled **wideth,** the e would make the i long. By dropping the e, one gets the phonically correct spelling **width.** The same applies to **wise + dom.** This gives **wisedom,** with a long i. However, the spelling with a dropped e, **wisdom,** is phonically correct, and is also "dictionary" correct.

In **true** + **ly**, giving **truely**, the e is unnecessary, as syllable division gives **tru ly**. Since the vowel ending an accentuated syllable is pronounced long, the correct spelling **truly** does not need the e to keep the u long.

In the case of **argue** + **ment**, giving **arguement** instead of the correct (dictionary) spelling **argument**, the e is not phonically necessary to keep the u long. Syllable division keeps the u long: **argu ment**. The u at the end of an accentuated syllable is pronounced long.

In the word **awe** + **ful**, giving **aweful**, the e is not needed for any phonic reason, and is simply dropped. **Aweful** and the correct spelling **awful** are pronounced exactly the same way.

Thus, of the sixteen words that do not follow the rule set forth at the beginning of this heading, eleven are seen to be phonic after all. Only the remaining five are truly unphonic.

Nine + **th** should be **nineth**, with the i long. However, the e is dropped with the i still pronounced long, making this an unphonic word, **ninth**.

Whole + **ly** should be **wholely**, with a long o. However, the e is dropped and the o still pronounced long, making this an unphonic word, **wholly**. But there is a shred of justification for the long o sound of o, since frequently the o is long before l as in words like old, bold, and told.

The three words **judgment**, **abridgment**, and **acknowledgment** should retain the e after the g to be phonically correct. This is because the g is pronounced soft, as if before the weak vowels (e, i, and u). The above words should be pronounced with a hard g from a phonic standpoint, but are not. This is another case of poor spelling getting to be so common that it becomes the "proper" spelling.

In words that end with a silent e, the addition of a suffix that begins with a vowel or a y usually causes the final e to be dropped:

$$
\begin{array}{llll}
\text{value} & + & \text{able} & = & \text{valuable} \\
\text{snuggle} & + & \text{ed} & = & \text{snuggled} \\
\text{simple} & + & \text{y} & = & \text{simply} \\
\text{argue} & + & \text{ing} & = & \text{arguing}
\end{array}
$$

admirable	icy	shady	desirable
scribbled	lacy	wobbly	excusable
advisable	spicy	tackled	excitable
encouraged	scary	trembled	continued
continuing	excited	admiring	trembling
encouraging	excused	arranged	arranging

The above rule holds for thousands of words. However, there are nineteen common words that do not follow this rule but are nevertheless phonic because they follow other equally valid phonic rules:

changeable	manageable	marriageable
knowledgeable	chargeable	

These words do not drop the silent e before the able ending because of the g. A g before e, i, or y is pronounced with the soft sound. In the above words, dropping the e puts the g before an a, and would change the g from a soft g to a hard g. This is why the silent e is retained. Please note the following words:

replaceable	noticeable	traceable
pronounceable	serviceable	

The silent e is retained before the <u>able</u> ending in order for the c to keep the s sound. C before e, i, and y has the sound of s. Before all other letters it has the sound of k. If the silent e were dropped, the c sound would change to a k sound because it would be before a letter that was not e, i, or y. Please note the following words:

courageous   outrageous   advantageous

If the silent e were dropped before the suffix **ous,** then the g would be before an o, and be required to take on the hard g sound. For this reason, the e is retained when adding the suffix **ous.**

Please note:
                canoe + ing = canoeing
                shoe   + ing = shoeing

The silent e here is not really a silent e but functions to make the o into a double o, thus giving the oo sound of soon and spoon. Thus, if the e were dropped, the o would have to take on the long sound and the word would not be understandable; canoing and shoing are not recognizable words.

In the word **hoe + ing = hoeing,** the root word is so short that to shorten it further would cause confusion. When one sees **hoing,** it is hard to tell what pronunciation is desired.

Consider the word **dye + ing = dyeing.** If it were spelled **dying,** it would mean something entirely different than putting a color into a cloth.

The same principle used in the word hoeing applies also to acre + age = acreage. The word is too short (acrage) to eliminate the e without causing it to become unrecognizable.

The last of the nineteen words that do not follow the rule in which the silent e is dropped before a suffix that begins with either y or a vowel is the word **mileage**. Again, if the e were dropped, the word is too short (milage) to be recognized for its basic meaning.

When a suffix is added to a word ending with a y, there are two simple rules. (1) Keep the final y when adding a suffix that begins with the letter i. (2) Before all other suffixes, change the letter y to i. Please note:

```
vary + ing = varying     qualify + ed  = qualified
vary + ed  = varied      qualify + ing = qualifying
```

The reason for this is in the nature of the letter y. Y has the aspect of a terminal sound, while the i has the aspect of a propelling sound. The y is used to ensure a pause before the i, so that two syllables will be sounded and there will not be a blending of a double i as occurs in the word skiing.

Some practice words follow. Please pay attention to the spelling, and see if the student can reconstruct the word minus the suffix. For example, luckily is lucky + ly.

busily	furious	emptiness	hungrily
steadily	heavily	occupying	occupied
mysterious	luckily	magnified	holiness
magnifying	studied	specified	studying
loneliness	various	modifying	modified
friendliness	glorious	liveliness	studious

A rather interesting rule occurs concerning the addition of the suffix **ly** to a word ending with **c**. Instead of adding ly, the proper suffix is **ally**. Please note, however, that the extra **al** of the **ally** suffix is not pronounced:

automatic	automatically	drastic	drastically
artistically		musically	critically
specifically		magically	frantically
electrically		basically	practically
economically		comically	magestically
scientifically		politically	systematically

The only exception to the above rule is the word publicly.

Please note that in syllabification the suffix is usually treated as a separate syllable.

walk	ing	state	ment	love	ly	advis	able
final	ly						

NOUN OR VERB?

One of the most basic principles of phonics is that a syllable is an independent part of a word. The pronunciation of one syllable will not affect the pronunciation of adjacent syllables. That which will have an effect on the word as a whole is the amount of stress given to each syllable. Stress emphasis on a syllable will change a voiceless consonant into a voiced counterpart, or change a schwa vowel sound into a full, long vowel sound.

Speech involves rhythm, and often this rhythm is critical in determining important accents upon syllables, essential to understanding. Nowhere is this better illustrated than in the use of the same word as a noun or as a verb. In this situation, it is the noun that has the accent on an early syllable, and the verb that has the accent on the last syllable. Please note:

Record
He bought a <u>record</u> at the store. Here the accent is on the first syllable, re'cord. Record is a noun.

Use the tape machine to <u>record</u> that. Here, the accent is on the second syllable, re cord'. Record is a verb.

Content
The <u>content</u> of the book is secret. Con'tent is a noun.
The children are <u>content</u> at last. Con tent' is a verb.

Convict
He is a <u>convict</u> in the state jail. Con'vict is a noun.
The jury did <u>convict</u> him of the crime. Con vict' is a verb.

Object
What is the <u>object</u> of your visit? Ob'ject is a noun.
I <u>object</u> to the tax increase. Ob ject' is a verb.

Rebel
He is known to be a <u>rebel</u>. Reb'el is a noun.
The troops did not <u>rebel</u>. Re bel' is a verb.

Excuse

What is your <u>excuse</u>? Excuse as a noun has a soft sound of s.

Please <u>excuse</u> me. Excuse as a verb has a voiced sound of s, sounded like the letter z, because the accent falls on the latter syllable and changes the s to a z sound.

Detail

Please note the <u>detail</u> in this painting. Detail as a noun is de'tail. The e is pronounced long, as are vowels that end an accentuated syllable.

Please <u>detail</u> your activities of last week. De tail' as a verb has a schwa e sound in accordance with the rule that unaccentuated syllables ending with a vowel are pronounced as a schwa, thus də tail' results.

As an optional exercise, the teacher may have the student write sentences in which the same word is used first as a noun and then as a verb, noting the accents and pronunciation changes between the same word used in these two different contexts. Here is a list:

abstract	collect	accent	annex	advance
contrast	address	export	retail	convert
conflict	conduct	detail	survey	consort
contract	contest	cement	combat	ferment
increase	subject	survey	extract	bargain
decrease	torment	permit	transfer	perfume

ACCENT AND THE DOUBLED CONSONANT

Not all words change stress emphasis when they are used as either nouns or verbs. In Level Two, it was shown that certain endings added to a word require that the consonant be doubled if the preceding vowel is to be kept short. The most common of these endings are ed and ing: commit, committed, committing. There is, however, one more condition to be considered regarding the doubling of the final consonant before the endings ed and ing. Please note:

refer refer_ring   color coloring

The word <u>refer</u> doubles the final consonant before a suffix beginning with a vowel. The word <u>color</u> changes to coloring without doubling the final consonant. Why?

The answer depends upon where the accent occurs in the word. There is a doubling of the final consonant of a word when adding a suffix that begins with a vowel only if:

(1) The vowel ends with a single consonant preceded by a vowel,
(2) The suffix begins with a vowel, and
(3) The word is accentuated on the last syllable.

The only new information in the above list is the third condition, concerning the accentuated syllable. Please note:

prefer	preferring	preferred	(pre fer')
honor	honoring	honored	(hon'or)
propel	propelled	propelling	(pro pel')
rumor	rumored	rumoring	(ru'mor)

Some additional words for the student to consider:

occur	occurring	occurred
confer	conferring	conferred
commit	committed	committing
differ	differed	differing
cancel	canceled	canceling
shovel	shoveled	shoveling
label	labeled	labeling
pilot	piloted	piloting
expel	expelled	expelling
acquit	acquitted	acquitting
patrol	patrolled	patrolling
control	controlled	controlling

PLURALS

In order to understand the phonic principles behind the formation of plurals, it is necessary to start with a short discussion of equivalent voiced and unvoiced consonants. In English, there are five such pairs:

Voiced		Unvoiced equivalent	
v	(vast)	f	(fast)
g	(gin)	k	(kin)
b	(bit)	p	(pit)
d	(dome)	t	(tome)
z	(zinc)	s	(sink)

These pairs of letters are equivalent in that if one uses the mouth position for a voiced consonant, but pronounces it without using the vocal cords, the unvoiced counterpart will be sounded, and vice-versa. This has previously been demonstrated in regard to the pairs f and v, s and z, and t and d. (of and off, for example).

In Reading Level One, it was noted that there are two pronunciations of the final s. After the unvoiced consonants f, k, p, and t, the s is pronounced voiceless:

cats   mats   ducks   racks   huffs   cuffs   hips
bumps

After voiced consonants, the s takes on its voiced equivalent which is the sound of z:

runs	tubs	wigs	rugs	ribs	digs	dogs
bells	hums	hogs	jogs	wins	hugs	lugs
hills	rugs	bugs

The reason for this lies in the nature of vocal cord vibration. Unvoiced consonants do not get the vocal cords vibrating in order to make their sound, and the vocal cords do not start up just to vibrate for one terminal sound. This is why the s is soft (unvoiced) after f, k, p, and t.

However, after a voiced consonant, the s cannot be pronounced in an unvoiced manner. In order for the speaker to pronounce the final s as an s (unvoiced), the preceding consonant must drop its voiced aspect. But if this is done, note what happens:

Pronounce **bags** with a soft s and it becomes **backs**. The same thing occurs with **tags** - it becomes **tacks**. **Bugs** becomes **bucks**.

Please look once more at the list of voiced and unvoiced consonants at the beginning of this section. The letter k is the unvoiced equivalent of g. This explains why one cannot pronounce any **ink** word without it sounding like **ingk**. Try pronouncing pink, stink, and think and they will always sound like "pingk", "stingk", and "thingk". This is because the vocalized consonant n converts the unvoiced consonant k into its voiced equivalent, g.

Cubs pronounced with an attempt to preserve the soft s becomes **cups**. **Tubs** becomes **tups**. **Cobs** becomes **cops**. The reason for this is that the equivalent unvoiced counterpart of b is p.

Try pronouncing **beds** with a soft s. It will sound like **bets**. **Pods** becomes **pots**. **Dads** becomes **dats**.

The plural of a noun is formed by adding s whenever the s unites readily with the word <u>without</u> forming an extra syllable.

boy boys   book books   uniform uniforms

picnics	answers	hinges	foes	times
promises	messages	forests	toys	doors
strangers	orchards	chances	chairs	lights

The addition of s to a noun is the most common way of forming the plural.

In words in which the s cannot readily unite, an es must be used to form the plural. This occurs after the words that end in s, x (ks), and the digraphs sh and ch. These are unvoiced sounds, and the s cannot be added on. Because an es is needed, an extra syllable results.

alias-aliases actress-actresses scratch-scratches
speeches   brushes   wishes   arches   boxes
branches   prefixes   suffixes   bushes   foxes
surpluses   compasses   reflexes   matches   gases
sandwiches   eyelashes   churches   marshes   mixes

Please note that when the ch is not a digraph, but is the sound of k with a silent h, then the plural takes just an s.

stomachs   monarchs   epochs

The most unusual plural is that which is sometimes formed after f and fe. In most cases, the plural simply adds an s:

cliff cliffs   dwarf dwarfs   giraffe giraffes
bailiffs   bluffs   briefs   chefs   gulfs
sheriffs   chiefs   griefs   clefs   cuffs
plaintiffs   reliefs   proofs   puffs   reefs
mischiefs   beliefs   whiffs   waifs   safes

However, in certain words in which the f or fe is preceded by a long vowel or an l, and the word is derived from a direct English source, the f and fe change to ves in forming the plural.

calf	calves	half	halves	elf	elves
life	lives	wife	wives	shelf	shelves
wolf	wolves	self	selves	thief	thieves
leaf	leaves	loaf	loaves	knife	knives

The words in the above list are examples of the unvoiced f becoming the voiced v. When this happens, the accent stress shifts to the end of the word. In a few words, however, the plural may be formed in either way:

wharf wharfs wharves scarf scarfs scarves

Nouns ending with y take their plurals in one of two ways. (1) When the word ends with y preceded by a vowel, add s:

alley	alleys	attorney	attorneys
boy	boys	pulley	pulleys

chimneys	donkeys	journeys	keys	kidneys
whiskeys	monkeys	trolleys	turkeys	valleys

(2) When the final y of the word is preceded by a consonant, the y is changed to an i and es is added to form the plural:

ally	allies	berry	berries
body	bodies	tragedy	tragedies

comedies	cities	skies	follies
countries	lilies	daisies	stories
quantities	juries	pastries	enemies
territories	ladies	luxuries	policies

This change in spelling for the plural is to avoid the pause aspect of the pronunciation of letter y. Letter i propels the sound so that the plural form ies makes only one syllable.

It was previously noted that the letter x does not have a sound of its own, but is pronounced with either the sound of **ks** or **gz.**

The **ks** sound:

mix   hex   fix   axle   oxen   extra   fox

The **gz** sound:

exact   exhaust   exist   example   exam   exude

Please note that ks is the unvoiced equivalent of gz. If there is a succeeding stressed vowel or a silent h, the unvoiced ks sound becomes the voiced gz.

MISCELLANEOUS

The best teachers work themselves out of a job by enabling their students to become self-reliant. It is the hope of the author that the teacher now feels that the student is ready to be on his own as far as reading phonically is concerned. Rather than just present rule after rule, the purpose has been to present a way of thinking about phonics. When new spelling patterns are encountered, it is anticipated that the student will think about them and try to make up a tentative rule of his own. New words encountered with the same spelling pattern will either enhance the theory or discredit it. Either way it will be a good exercise. It is clearly impossible to cover every contingency as far as phonics and spelling is concerned. What is possible is a way of thinking, so that the student has a method to use when trying to synthesize order out of seeming chaos.

As an example of the above problem solving, consider something that was not covered in the text: the **sc** combination of words like **scissors, scenery, science, ascend, and descent.** The student encountering this consonant combination already knows one important thing from the teacher, and that is how the consonant combination is to be pronounced. It will take an enlongated s sound. Now, the question is why. Is there a consistent rule? The c before the e or the i gives a clue. C has only a k or an s sound, and the s sound appears before the e, i, and y. So, the sc is pronounced ss, and scissors could be just as well spelled ssissors. However, no word ever begins with ss, and the sc spelling is used because this was the spelling of the Latin root. The student going through this thought process will have discovered a guide behind the spelling and pronunciation of words with sc before e or i, rather than trying to memorize isolated words and hoping that somehow the subconscious will put things in order.

By thinking about what seem to be utterly terrible or inconsistent spellings, some reason for them can usually be ascertained. Consider the word **courteous.** It could just as well be spelled "kerties" or "cortieus". At one time all the vowels in the word courteous were pronounced, but now only a basic few are sounded. The initial o is dropped, and the ur sound is a schwa er sound. This results in a **ker** sound for the initial syllable. (Note that the k must be used before the e to get the k sound.) The second syllable, the **te,** makes sense as it stands. Considering the **eous,** it is already known or should have been surmised that in modern English one never pronounces three vowels in a row. One has to go, and in this case it will be the o. So, courteous becomes understandable if one simply drops the two o's and pronounces it "curteus".

It is interesting to note that in the spelling <u>beauty</u>, there are three vowels in a row. One must be dropped, and here it is the a. However, one can make a case for the a being there in order to keep the e long and preventing it from reverting to the schwa sound. The French used to pronounce all the vowels in the eau combination but have now shortened the sound to a simple o, as in the now-English word beau. The point is that an inquiring student can usually arrive at a plausible reason for the spelling and pronunciation of any word in English. A helpful guide is to know that at one time in the past <u>all</u> the letters were pronounced. With some words, some of the letters that should be there for pronunciation have been dropped over time while the original pronunciation of the word still persists. The opposite situation occurs in the case of silent letters, those letters persisting in spite of not being pronounced. Some scholarship into "unphonic" words is a very educational pastime.

A few more "tough" words:

<u>Cautious.</u> The pronunciation is not difficult, as the au = aw, and the ti = sh. The o before the u in the ou combination at the end of a word is usually dropped. It could be spelled "cawshus", but this spelling does no justice to the development of the word from the Latin <u>cautio</u>.

In <u>language</u> and <u>distinguish</u> the spellings could be "langwage" and "distingwish" and a person reading these words phonically would understand the word. It has already been noted that the w is a double u, and therefore the substitution of the u for a w is justified in spelling.

There are changes in pronunciation of some words with lengthening of the word. In the word <u>initial</u> the ti has the sh sound, and the word is pronounced "inishal", both i's being schwa sounds. However, in the word <u>initiation</u> the t alone carries the sh sound, and the i is sounded with a hiatus before the next vowel, the a, resulting in the pronunciation "inishiashun". A phonic reader notes things like this, and usually does well in writing these spelling-bee horrors.

There have been many attempts to reform the English spelling system to conform with modern pronunciations. If spellings were changed to reflect local pronunciations, it would not be long before the printed word in England would be almost unintelligible to the reader in Australia or in the southern United States, for example. The invention of moveable type by Gutenberg (1398-1468) with the subsequent dissemination of language in printed form, was the prime factor in freezing the spelling patterns, a process generally complete by 1650. For the most part, the advantages of retaining our current spelling system far outweigh the disadvantages of a system where everyone spells as he wishes. It is comforting to be able to read literature that is 350 years old with only the minor distractions of older spellings like **publick** and **musick,** and words containing now obsolete doubled consonants and final e's.

It is remarkable that the alphabet has been invented only once. Every alphabetic system in use today can be traced back to the Phoenician alphabet. The idea has been passed on from culture to culture, from its inception in the tenth century B. C. until the present. It continues now as illiterate peoples are having their spoken language recorded for them and the alphabet taught to them by dedicated persons such as missionaries. The ancient Egyptians had developed a picture-symbol system of twenty-four signs that represented the consonant sounds of their language.

However, they used this primarily to record the sounds of the names of visiting foreign dignitaries, something they could not represent adequately with pictographs. It was left to the Phoenicians to take the giant step to the development of a complete sound-symbol system, an alphabet. The knowledge of the alphabet spread to the Greeks on one hand, and to the Brahmans of India on the other hand. The latter lead to the Sanskrit alphabet and all its derivatives. Through the Greek lineage came all the alphabets of the world based on the Greco-Roman model, including, of course, the one you are reading right now.

The final thought of this book is as follows: there are no really "unphonic" words. There are just fossilized misspellings and uninformed teachers. There is only one proper way to teach and learn English, and it is by the use of phonics.

SUMMARY OF READING LEVEL FIVE
PHONIC RULES

1.   Consonants may have a different sound before the vowel u. In the tu and du combinations, the t and d take on the digraph ch sound: nature, picture, schedule, gradual.

The s before u may take on the sh sound: sugar, sure, insurance.

The s before u can take on a z sound if it follows a vowel: treasure, measure, leisure.

2.   When the ti, si, and ci combinations are followed by a vowel which is in the same syllable, these combinations give the sh sound: mention, pension, facial, ambition, occasion, erosion, suspicion.

3.   Prefixes are added to a word without dropping any letters: reenter, dissolve, unnatural, misspell, co-owner, disappear, co-editor, rejoin.

4.   A syllable break occurs between the prefix and the main word:

co exist   un important   re cover

5.   A suffix beginning with a consonant adds onto the word directly:

final + ly = finally   improve + ment = improvement

In words ending with a silent e, suffixes beginning with a vowel cause the final e to be dropped:

value + able = valuable   snuggle + ed = snuggled

simple + y = simply   argue + ing = arguing.

In words ending with letter y, keep the final y in adding a suffix that begins with letter i: vary + ing = varying,   qualify + ing = qualifying.

Before all other suffixes, change the y to i:

vary + ed = varied   qualify + ed = qualified.

6.   The suffix is usually treated as a separate syllable:
        walk ing   love ly   advis able   state ment
7.   In words of the same spelling used as either a noun or
a verb, the nouns are stressed on initial syllables and the
verbs are stressed on final syllables:
     What is the object (ob'ject) of your visit?
     I object (ob ject') to the tax increase.
8.   Suffixes beginning with vowels usually cause the final
vowel of the main word to be pronounced long if only one
consonant separates the vowel from the suffix:
        hoping liked diner super planed taping
     If the final vowel is to be kept short, a doubled
consonant is needed:
        hopping dinner supper planned tapping
     However, if the accent does not fall on the last
syllable of the word, the final consonant is not doubled
before the addition of the suffix. Please note:
confer' conferring propel' propeller   control' controlling
hon'or honoring   shov'el shoveling   ru'mor   rumored
9.   Most nouns form plurals by adding s. This s is
pronounced as an s (unvoiced) after the unvoiced consonants
f, k, p, and t:
              cats   ducks   huffs   hips
     After all other consonants, the s is pronounced as a z:
   runs tubs hills dogs hums hogs rugs doors keys

     Words that end with s, x, and the digraphs sh and ch
form the plural by adding es:

        speeches   foxes   brushes   actresses

10.   Words ending in f or fe usually add s to form the plural:

      dwarfs   giraffes   beliefs   serfs   proofs   sheriffs

However, when the word is of pure English derivation and the f or fe is preceded by a long vowel or l, the f changes to v, and es is added:

      calves   elves   wolves   wives   selves

11.   Words ending with y add s in the plural if the y is preceded by a vowel:

      chimneys   keys   kidneys   boys   valleys

If the y is preceded by a consonant, then the y is changed to an i and es is added:

      berries   bodies   cities   skies   juries

LEVEL FIVE STORIES

1. THE TREASURE

2. THE TOY STORE

3. THE DETECTIVE AGENCY

4. STARTING SUPPER

5. THE COUNTRY CLUB

The stories in Level Five contain all the phonic difficulties that are found in English, save the most exotic. If there are any difficulties in reading any of the words, please refer back to the appropriate sections and re-do the exercises. The stories in this book are designed to teach phonic skills. They are not specifically designed to enhance reading comprehension, and therefore do not employ advanced writing techniques such as use of the subjunctive or the use of metaphore.

THE TREASURE

It was a warm, summer day. Louis and Raymond were on their way to the cave that they had discovered yesterday. They were both quite nervous. They had been digging in the cave and discovered a buried treasure. It wasn't the kind of treasure that pirates leave, like gold coins and precious stones and pearl necklaces. It was buried money, mostly in paper bills and some coins. It was a lot of money, thousands and thousands of dollars.

Yesterday they were too scared to do anything but put the money back in the chest and cover it with dirt and stones. They had intended to tell the sheriff about it, but they didn't trust him. Louis's dad had said that the sheriff was a bit of a crook and he was sorry that the people had ever elected him. He was sure that the sheriff would not be reelected the next time. The boys didn't want the sheriff taking the treasure they had found and keeping it for himself. The boys decided to mention it to no one.

They had spent the morning in the library looking at old newspapers. They were sure the money was the loot from some robbery. They were curious enough to look at all the papers for a few years back. Big robberies are usually reported on the front page, so they looked at just the front pages at the library's newspaper collection. They found nothing to indicate the money was taken from any nearby bank or other local establishment.

They concluded that an eccentric person must have buried the money in the cave and forgotten about it. Anyway, they felt it was a case of "finders keepers". If they told about the money, a lot of people would claim it and it might be years before they got to keep any of it.

They decided that the safest thing to do was to bring back the money a little at a time. Then they would not arouse suspicion. They did not mention the money to anyone and planned to make up a pirate-type map and hide the money in a lot of different places so that if anyone found one part of the money, they would still have the rest.

But now they were suspicious of things they had ignored before. Was anyone following them? Did anyone see them leave the cave yesterday? They decided to be extra cautious. Louis went to the top of the hill that overlooked the cave and took his binoculars and a bell along. Raymond went on into the cave to get a portion of the money. If Louis saw anything suspicious, he was to ring the bell to warn Raymond that someone was coming. Raymond was then to take what he could, cover over what was left in the cave, and get out quickly.

It worked perfectly. No one seemed to notice them at all. Raymond had taken only a small portion of the money and it was over a thousand dollars. The boys had never seen so much money before. They touched it over and over again, still not entirely convinced that it was real and not counterfeit or something like that.

The only way to know for sure if it was real was to spend some of it. They hid a substantial portion in their treehouse and took the rest to go shopping. Raymond bought a new pair of sneakers. The saleslady took the twenty dollar bill and didn't even look at it a second time. Then Louis bought a pair of roller skates. Again, the sales clerk took the money without a second glance at the twenty dollar bill. Raymond thought that he could use a new bike and picked out a nice one that was a bit expensive. He gave the clerk two fifty dollar bills. To the relief of the boys, the clerk took them and put them in his cash register without any fuss. He had looked at them carefully for a moment, but nothing more. Apparently the money was real all right.

Raymond suggested that they try to spend one of the hundred dollar bills. They knew that people who knew them would wonder where they got so much money. So they made up a plan to look like rich kids. They used some of their twenties to buy nice clothing, something that their parents never got for them because it was too expensive. Then they went to the other part of town to an exclusive store that sold only expensive articles. There they saw a portable television set run by batteries that would be perfect for their treehouse. It was almost four hundred dollars. They ordered it with all the authority they could put into their voices, expecting that the clerk would tell them to scram and play somewhere else. But their plan worked. Somehow, expensive clothes do things for people. The clerk was very nice when they handed her the four one hundred dollar bills. She even called a cab for them when they told her that they would like to take the set along with them and not have to wait for delivery. They were amazed at how nice people are to kids who have a lot of money and are dressed well.

They had the cab stop about a block away from their houses. They didn't want their parents to get suspicious. Raymond took the television set to the treehouse by going around the back way, through the yard. Louis went to the store to get some comic books and snacks. The boys enjoyed themselves in their treehouse and were careful not to turn up the volume too high so that their parents could hear that they had a T. V. set in the treehouse. The boys enjoyed the pleasure of a life of leisure.

They made up a schedule for getting all the money out of the cave. Every day they went back to the cave and got more of the money. They hid most of what they brought back to the treehouse, and spent only a portion. Soon the treehouse was filled with expensive things. They had nice furniture. They had an oriental rug on the floor. There were pictures and tapestries on the walls. Each boy had a silk bathrobe. Their slippers were furlined. Stacks of comic books were in the corners. They had cans of exotic things like smoked salmon and caviar which they didn't find especially delicious but had bought because they saw some rich people getting them in a fancy delicatessen. Eventually they had all the money out of the cave and hidden in places of their own.

Their parents noticed that the boys usually didn't seem hungry at suppertime and barely touched their food. What the parents didn't know was that the boys were eating out at expensive restaurants each lunchtime.

Sooner or later people begin to get supicious. Some of the clerks got curious about the boys. One man began to follow them. The boys didn't know it, but he was one of the thieves who had stolen the money that they had found. There were two crooks who had robbed a bank and had an argument about dividing up the loot. One had hidden the money so that the other could not find it. Later, one of the thieves had committed another robbery and was caught by the police and sent off to jail. The man following the boys was the thief who had been cheated out of his share of the loot by the crook who was now in jail. The bank they had robbed was in a city in the next county, and the story had not appeared on the front page of the local newspaper.

But the boys' parents had been noticing too many unusual things to contain their curiosity. There were expensive bikes parked under the treehouse. The boys were never hungry at suppertime. All they ever did was spend the day going around the city or staying in the treehouse. Raymond's dad decided to get some answers to his questions by taking a look in the treehouse. But the crook was already there, looking for the loot. Raymond's dad saw the crook first and took away the ladder and called the police. The crook was

captured. He could not get down because the tree-house was too high off the ground and he would have gotten hurt if he jumped.

The sheriff responded to the police call. He put the ladder back and ordered the man to come down. The sheriff recognized the man as a criminal who was wanted in connection with a bank robbery that had taken place in the next county the year before. The sheriff put handcuffs on the crook and made him stay in his squad car. When the sheriff and the boys' parents saw all the things in the treehouse, they guessed the connection between the crook's being there and all the stuff the boys had gotten.

The boys confessed what had happened. They had found the money in a cave. They told that they had looked in the newspapers and did not see anything about a major robbery and had concluded that some rich old person had put the money there and forgotten about it. The sheriff was mad that they had not reported the finding of the money to him. The boys told their dads that they mistrusted the sheriff, but no one said that to the sheriff directly.

The bank president was notified about the discovery of the loot and came over to see the boys. He had a list of the serial numbers of the money and it matched the money that the sheriff had found in the treehouse. It was the bank's money. The boys gave the map of their buried treasure to the men and then cooperated with them and helped dig up the missing portion of the loot.

The president of the bank was delighted to get most of the money back and made the suggestion that the boys could keep what they had already spent as a reward. This made the sheriff mad, as he felt they should be punished for not coming to him with their discovery in the first place. But the sheriff couldn't do anything to the boys because little kids aren't supposed to automatically know that when large sums of money are found the police must be notified. The parents gave the boys a long lecture and pointed out to them that that crook might have hurt them to get his loot back. The boys now realized how dangerous it can be to keep money that isn't yours and promised to never do anything like that again in the future. Still, they were pleased to have such a nicely furnished treehouse and all those other things they had bought while they felt like rich kids.

THE TOY STORE

Elizabeth and Donald are siblings. They consider themselves especially lucky because their father likes to fix things. He has a fully equipped workroom that contains the best tools for doing unusual things like making fancy furniture. He built garage doors that automatically open and close at the push of a button from inside the house or from inside the car. He built kitchen cabinets with variable width shelves. He built the children a child-sized ping-pong table that was easy for them to use. He built Elizabeth a doll house that had a lot of nice miniature furniture and was so detailed that it even had little light fixtures that were permanently attached to the ceilings. Everything was measured carefully so that all things matched. There were even functioning extension cords so that she could plug in table lamps to a main power supply that was attached to the back of the doll house. Elizabeth was pleased to get that as a birthday present. She would much rather have something that her dad made than the things that were for sale in the stores. He had also built some nice toys for Donald. Some of the toys were trucks and cars which had doors that opened, a horn that actually made a honk when activated, and lights that turned on and off. One car even had an exhaust pipe that made a special sound when the car was pushed along the floor. Some of the cars and trucks had battery operated motors. Donald liked the toys his father made very much because he thought they were of better quality than the toys at the toy stores. It was a pleasure to play with the toys that dad made because they didn't fall apart with heavy use.

What was especially nice for the kids is that dad could fix any toy that got broken. If a doll's arm got severed, he could fix it so well that it would be stronger than it was initially, and would never break in the same spot again. Because he used only the best paints and varnishes, it was usually impossible to tell where the fractures had been. Dad even had some electronic equipment. He had a soldering gun and lots of wires and spare light bulbs. It was easy for him to fix the electronic and mechanical toys that are so frequently found in stores these days.

Donald especially liked to watch his dad fix the toys that contained lights and motors and used electronic circuits run by batteries. Elizabeth liked to watch him fix dolls and stuffed animals. He could also do invisible mending so well that it looked as if there had never been a tear or rip in any cloth. He used special needles that allowed him to sew from the back side of a cloth, and he always took the trouble to match his thread with the exact color of the cloth. Mom said that he should sew his own clothes too because he was such a good tailor, but he never did anything like that. Clothes were always left to mother to fix.

Dad was an insurance salesman and never had the intention of making or fixing things as a profession. It was only a hobby for him. The satisfaction he got from making his children happy with things he made was sufficient reward for doing what he did.

One day the children found some discarded toys in a trash can by the curb. They were nice toys, but each had a little thing broken. The kids were amazed that someone would throw away an expensive toy just because they were too lazy to find out what was wrong with it. Since the toys were left in a trash can, the kids didn't think it was wrong for them to take them home with them and see if they could be fixed up.

Donald took the robot toy apart and found that all it needed to be put back in perfect working order was for a wire to be soldered to the battery connection. Elizabeth found that a doll was easily repaired by glueing on a new wig and washing the doll's dress. It was the same with all the other toys. Even though they had no instructions about the construction of the toys, it was not hard to fix them if they simply thought about how they might be designed to function.

The kids got an idea for a business of their own. They would start a second-hand toy store. They began by putting up posters advertising that they would buy old and broken toys. It was not long before kids came over to their house with wagonloads of discarded toys that were intended for the trash heap. Donald offered prices that ranged from twenty-five cents to two dollars for an entire wagonload and most of the kids accepted it. Some of their friends gave them toys which they considered junk. Elizabeth and Donald were glad they didn't have to pay much for these old toys because some of them were in a truly awful condition. After all, if something is going to be thrown away, anything paid for it is like finding money. It was quite a mixture of things that they bought. Roller skates with the straps missing. A racing car that had a remote control that did not transmit signals like it was supposed to do. A tricycle with two flat tires. A doll carriage with a wheel missing. There were lots of dolls that had terribly torn clothing or damaged parts. Some things the kids would not buy, things that were too damaged or required parts that were simply too difficult to come by. In this case the other kids usually left the broken toys anyway and Donald often used a portion of this stuff as a source of parts to fix other toys. They had emptied their piggy banks to pay for this collection of junk that they anticipated turning into something that other kids would want. After all, it is the condition and function of a toy that determines its attractiveness. If the kids could take trash and turn it into treasure, then there might possibly be a nice profit to be made.

They used dad's workshop to make the toys functional again. They used the tricks they had learned from dad to make the toys look even better than they did when they were new. Weak spots were reenforced. Batteries were replaced and wire connections made especially strong so that they

could stand rigorous movements. Everything was at least painted or touched up with special matching paints of all colors so that no seams were visible. Elizabeth had laundered the dolls' clothing so that it looked and smelled new.

A neighbor was having a garage sale. He gave the children permission to hold their toy sale in his garage along with his own sale. In their rural neighborhood, it was common for grownups to get rid of unwanted and unneeded articles by

selling them from their garages. The kids put up
some posters that advertised the fact that there
were things for children at this garage sale. It
was a special two-in-one sale, something for the
adults and something for the kids.

It was a big success. The best customers for
the toys were not the kids but the parents. Many
parents were disgusted at the high prices and low
quality of many of the toys that are sold in
regular stores. It is not unusual for toys to be

broken on the very first day the kid plays with them. Elizabeth and Donald had taken a trip to the local toy stores about town and noted the prices. They charged only half as much. Considering that they had bought the damaged toys for almost nothing and sold them at good prices, they made a very nice profit.

And so, a business was launched. Donald and Elizabeth had bought what some considered only junk and sold it for what others considered treasure. The difference in price, minus the work and material put into the toys, was their profit. It seemed that everyone was pleased, but this was not the case. One of the neighbors owned the large toy store in the shopping center and noted that his business was being affected by the loss of customers to Donald and Elizabeth. He complained to the mayor that he was the victim of unfair competition. He had to pay taxes and get a lot of permits and follow all the rules that the city imposes on businesses operating within the city limits. Why should children be exempt just because they are children? After all, they are operating at an advantage by operating out of their garage while he has to pay rent. The mayor consulted with the city attorney who checked the law books. The mayor was told that the children were in violation of city laws, and that he had to make them close their business if they did not get a whole lot of city permits and pay special taxes. The mayor called the kids' dad and told him that he had no choice but to enforce the city rules and insist that they stop their business.

A reporter for the newspaper thought that this was an interesting story and put it in the paper, along with a picture of Elizabeth and Donald repairing some old toys. Other newspapers copied the story, and people came from the television stations to do special reports for the evening news. Soon everyone in the entire state had heard about their business, and how the owner of the large toy store in the shopping center was trying to get the police to make two children stop competing with him. People got so mad at that toy store owner that soon no one came to his store at all.

It didn't take long for the toy store owner to drop his complaint. He went to the newspapers and told the reporters that he was only kidding, that he didn't really mean to make any trouble for the kids. He said that he realized that children should be encouraged to learn about doing useful things that could help them earn a living when they grew up. The reporters put his picture in the newspaper, and printed his apology about causing so much trouble for Elizabeth and Donald. The mayor told the reporters that he did not have to enforce the rules about businesses if there were no complaints. So, the kids could resume their used toy business. The toy store owner even went to their house and offered them a job of repairing toys for him, toys that arrived at his shop defective. It was cheaper to have an expert repair them rather than send them back to the manufacturer. The kids accepted his offer, and did the repair work for him. In return, they were sure that they labeled all their toys as being used, so that no one would think that they were selling the same thing as the owner of the toy store. All his toys had never been played with, and were new. People who wanted new things for their children went to the toy store, and people who wanted toys at a bargain price went to Elizabeth and Donald's garage. Now, everyone seemed pleased with this arrangement, especially Elizabeth and Donald. They had discovered for themselves what successful businessmen had known for years. It is not so much the hard work that gets a business to be successful as much as it is the ideas and good will behind the business.

THE DETECTIVE AGENCY

Jonathan started the Kids' Detective Agency, which he advertised as the only one of its kind in the whole world. He wasn't certain about that because he didn't know how to check and be sure that there weren't similar detective agencies somewhere. But he thought he was safe with this claim, as probably no one else would take the trouble to prove him wrong.

His first job came from his mother. It was to find out how the family dog was getting out of the yard. The neighbors were complaining that their dog Hero was digging in all the flower patches around the block. Jonathan found a hole that Hero had dug under the fence behind the lilac bushes. He dug the hole deeper and lined it with chicken wire before filling it in again, which was certain to discourage Hero from digging there again. That took care of the Case of the Escaping Dog, which was the way it was listed in his Solved file. He earned a dollar for his effort.

Gradually people other than his parents called him to do little chores. Usually he was to go to the playground and find out why some children weren't home when they were supposed to be. Often he was given the job of looking for lost cats and dogs. Once in a while he got the job to go to the post office and inquire why someone's package or piece of registered mail hadn't arrived yet. He didn't mind these little jobs as they were useful in keeping him busy until something important turned up, which was bound to happen some day.

One day the bank got robbed. Jonathan went to the police station to get the job of finding the crook. He was disappointed when he found out that they wouldn't hire him because he was too young. He thought he was better than everybody else in solving crimes because he had read every crime book in the public library.

He made up business cards. He called himself Sherlock. Who would ever have consulted Sherlock Holmes if his name had been Jonathan Holmes? He felt the name added luster to his agency.

His big business break occurred after a rash of burglaries hit his neighborhood. The police seemed bored with such investigations and were content to simply fill out reports that the home-owners could file with their insurance companies. The police didn't seem to think that they would ever catch the burglar and basically they only went through the motions of trying to solve the crimes. But Jonathan thought that there was nothing mysterious about these crimes and that they were solveable if a little effort was used. He got a detailed description of the things taken in the robberies and went around to all the pawnshops in town. There he found most of the stolen items. He got a description of the person who pawned these items and rode around the neighborhood on his bicycle looking for him. He soon realized that this was the hard way to find the thief and devised a special trap that would attract the crook and make him come forth.

He heard that his next-door neighbors were going away for a short vacation. He collected junk mail and got a pile of newspapers and folded them to look like the paperboy had them ready to throw on the lawns of his customers. After the neighbors left, Jonathan put the junk mail on the porch and scattered the newspapers on the lawn. It looked as if no one had been home for at least a week. He then set up his electric eyes in the front and back yards. These were special intruder detection devices that he had gotten in one of the electronic gadget stores. A beam of light is directed from one box to the other. If that beam is interrupted, it trips an electronic circuit that sets off a remote alarm. He ran the wires across the yard and through the fence into his own yard. From there he ran the wires up the side of his house and through the window into his room. His room had a window that overlooked the neighbor's house and he could see what was going on if a buzzer sounded from the light beam being interrupted. To make sure that he could prove that anyone caught was really a burglar, he put special powder on the door knobs and window sills. It was invisible in ordinary light, but glowed under florescent light.

It happened the very first night. Jonathan's buzzer went off at about ten o'clock. He looked from his window and saw a man going around the house, trying the doors and windows to see if any had been left unlocked. Jonathan called the police, and then got his camera. He sneaked from his house to the fence that separated the two yards, his and the neighbors. He saw the man prying open a window with a crowbar. The man heard the police siren approaching and turned to run. Jonathan called "Hey, you" to attract the man's attention so that he would look in his direction. As soon as the man did so, Jonathan pressed the shutter button on his camera which made the flash go off. It blinded the burglar so that he could not see where he was going. Jonathan yelled to the policeman who got out of the squad car that there was a burglar in the back yard and made a gesture to indicate where he was. It was easy to capture him, because he was still partially blinded by the camera flash. He had thrown the crowbar into the bushes so that the police wouldn't have any evidence that he was trying to break into houses.

Of course, the man used an excuse that he was really only taking a short-cut, and that he wasn't a burglar. Jonathan recovered the crowbar from the bushes. The man denied that the tool was his and insisted that he had no intention of trying to break into the house. But after Jonathan showed the police that the man's hands glowed under his special ultraviolet light, and showed them that he had put that special powder on the doors and windows, the police took him away to the station. They were going to test the crowbar to see if any of the burglar's fingerprints were on it. Jonathan went along in the second police car that had arrived shortly after the first. He showed

the police detectives his Polaroid picture of the
man prying the window, and told them that his
description matched that of the man who had pawned
the loot taken from the other robberies. The man
was booked into jail as a robbery suspect. The
police investigated, and all the recently pawned
items were traceable to the suspect that they had
apprehended. The people felt fortunate that they
got their possessions back, and the police were
finally able to write Case Solved on their many
reports of residential burglary investigations.
The crook was officially booked into the county
jail to await trial for suspicion of burglary in
connection with all those residential robberies.
Everyone arrested is presumed innocent until
proven guilty, but with all the evidence that
Jonathan had accumulated, there could be no doubt
what the verdict would be after the trial. Indeed, the crook felt that the police had such a
sufficiently strong case against him that he
pleaded guilty in the hope of getting a lighter
sentence from the judge.

Jonathan was a hero to all except his next-
door neighbors. They didn't like it that he used
their property as bait. But after the police
chief told them that they would probably have been
robbed soon anyway, they changed their attitude
toward Jonathan. The police found a list of intended houses and commercial businesses in the
burglar's pocket, and they were on that list.
There was no question that Jonathan had saved them
from having their property burglarized. Then they
joined in the praise of Jonathan and even began

calling him Sherlock like all the other people in the neighborhood were now doing. Indeed, Jonathan could hardly walk down the street that he wasn't invited into a house for pastries and soda. He was especially pleased to mark his <u>Burglary</u> file as Case Closed, Officially Solved.

The only other problem was a complaint from Jonathan's mother that he had needlessly exposed himself to danger by taking the burglar's picture. Jonathan agreed that it would have been better if he had set up the camera in a tree and used a trip wire to activate the camera. Then he would have been a safe distance from the burglar at all times. He promised to do this in any similar future cases.

The best reward was being made an honorary police detective. He got no reward money for his efforts, but that didn't really matter. He was allowed to go along with the police investigators and see how they went about investigating crimes. He thought this was a nice gesture on the part of the chief of police, but he didn't even suspect the real reason he was given this special privilege. Jonathan had shown up the detective division as being generally lazy and indifferent. By having Jonathan on the case, the chief was sure that his men would try to set an example and be more efficient and really try to solve crimes.

STARTING SUPPER

Cynthia liked to cook. As far back as she could remember, she was fascinated that different foods tasted differently. She was impressed with the methods that her mother used to change the taste of even the same foods, such as by adding special herbs and spices and cooking in different ways like frying, boiling, broiling, roasting, basting, and so forth.

At first, Cynthia was entrusted to prepare the salad and the salad dressing. Then her mother let her do things like make up her own soup concoctions. Later she was allowed to do things like shop in the farmers' market for the fresh vegetables. She went on to being entrusted with preparing the vegetables and gradually began cooking the main course itself, which was usually a variety of meat, fish, or poultry. She was never satisfied with anything bland. Her motto was something on the order of "If it's worth eating, it's worth making it taste good". Her dad said that he could never tell which of his ladies prepared what portion of the meal because it all tasted exquisite. Cynthia liked it when her dad called her a lady even though she was only eleven years old. It made her feel important and try even harder to impress him with her culinary skill.

Eventually Cynthia was cooking for guests who came to dinner. It was hard for her mother to be both the cook and the hostess at the same time and she welcomed Cynthia's help. It was not long before everyone in the neighborhood knew what a marvelous cook Cynthia was, and she began trading recipes with the grownups just like she was a regular housewife herself.

Before she realized it, Cynthia was engaged in a little business. Neighbors would often ask her to help them out with the cooking whenever they had parties for dinner guests. She would get a nice cash payment for her services. Then she began to get commissions to plan the menu and get the food for things like wedding parties, graduation celebrations, and baby christenings. She could work on these big parties only if they were held on weekend afternoons because she still had to get to bed early enough to get sufficient sleep to be ready for school on weekdays.

Her customers began entrusting her with everything, which meant that she planned the entire menu and even went to the store and bought all the ingredients. She often arranged to get extra silverware and table linens if needed. Whenever the party was for a lot of people, she got her friends to help, and she supervised the other girls. It was truly a business, one that got her a nice sum of money. Her dad was pleased at her industry, but told her that it was more important that she get a good education before thinking of going into a full-time business of her own after she finished high school. He didn't object to what she was doing as long as it didn't interfere with her school work.

One day a neighbor asked Cynthia if she could start her supper for her. The woman and her husband both had jobs. With both spouses working, it is hard for the lady of the house to come home and get a supper prepared for her husband and children early enough so that they won't complain that they have to wait so long to eat. Also, the kids never seem to start doing their homework until after supper, and with a late meal it it always a hurry-up situation that doesn't produce good results. The neighbor's family was tired of T. V. dinners and fast food. Cynthia thought the idea was interesting, and said that she would give it a try. She went to the neighbor's house about four in the afternoon and got things started. She put a small roast in the oven and set the temperature and timer so that it would be finished at six o'clock. She then got the vegetables prepared and placed them in the appropriate cooking pots on the stove, ready to be turned on when the neighbor got home about five-thirty. She did the same with the potatoes. There was a salad already made and in the refrigerator, and all that was necessary for serving was the addition of the salad dressing, which was in a jar next to the salad bowl. For dessert, a pie was in the lower oven, ready to be heated when the main meal was served.

It worked out so well that she got a regular after-school job. The neighbor felt that Cynthia was a big help and yet there was that element of not everything being done by someone else. The

lady of the house controlled things, put the final
finishing touches on the meal, and served it herself. It was an ideal situation for a working
wife. The only problem for Cynthia was that she
didn't have sufficient time to help her own mother
like she had done before. Her mother didn't mind,
because now she had control of her own kitchen
again, which was fine with her. Other neighbors
heard what Cynthia was doing and wanted her to do
the same thing for them. It was not possible for
her to be in more than one place at a time, so she
thought up a plan. She got together a group of
her friends and started a business which they
called Starting Supper. Cynthia was the one who
really knew about cooking, and set herself up as
the supervisor. She got a girl to go to each of
the customers' houses after school. Cynthia went
from house to house and supervised the preparation
of the supper. Her friends, who were now her
employees too, did the easy things like peeling
potatoes and washing the salad greens. Cynthia
added the spices and prepared the sauces and decided on the cooking time for each course and each
item. All the working housewives had to do was
add any little touch of their own and then serve
the food, just as if they had done the whole meal
themselves. If a customer wanted menu planning
and grocery shopping, that was an extra cost.

The best job is the one that you enjoy and
gets you money at the same time. Cynthia had to
limit her clients to people whose houses were
within easy walking distance of her own house.
She expanded her business only to the extent of

preparing desserts in her own kitchen and furnishing them upon request. This was all the extras she could provide during the school year. When summer vacation came, she planned to do more extras like preparing exotic dishes from foreign cookbooks.

Cynthia's mom was pleased at the success of her business and made little aprons for Cynthia and her employees. They had the initials SS sewed on them, which stood for Starting Supper, the name of their business. Cynthia's mom was always available to give advice and even helped out on those rare occasions when Cynthia was sick and couldn't do her usual supervising. This was a big asset, as no customer was ever disappointed.

Everyone seemes to have both friends and enemies, which happens no matter what you do. Cynthia soon found an easy way to find out who of her acquaintances were her friends and who were her enemies. Her friends were glad for her success. Her enemies were jealous and hoped that she'd mess up and that her business would fail. Indeed, some of the girls who didn't like Cynthia decided to deliberately create trouble for her.

Her enemies made copies of her aprons, even sewing the initials SS on them. They went to houses that were just beyond Cynthia's neighborhood and solicited business at a very low price. They represented themselves as Cynthia's employees. The price was so low that no one could really work for so little money, but the neighbors' didn't think about that. Most people nowadays are on a tight budget, and Cynthia's enemies were interested in getting hired, not in making a profit. These girls were spoilers, girls who were interested in discrediting Cynthia. They would rather tear down another's good achievement than strive to match it.

Then the tricks began. These imitation SS girls, Cynthia's enemies, messed up the ladies' kitchens and made suppers so bad that no one could actually eat them. The vegetables were over-cooked, the meat was burned, the salad was made of greens that belonged in the garbage can and not on a supper table. Some girls used so much pepper on the food that it actually made them sneeze to just sniff the food. They purposely spilled things all over the stove and on the floor. They left the refrigerator door open so that all the food inside got warm and the ice cream melted and dripped all over the floor. They set the temperature of the oven to 550 degrees which not only burned the food but also heated up the house to the point that it was very uncomfortable. They made a pudding out of eggs and vinegar and purposely left the egg-shells in the concoction. They made a pie using dog food. They put marbles instead of fruit in the jello and used shaving cream for the topping. They found a dead mouse and put it in the juice pitcher. They used shoe polish for salad dressing and purposely put it on the salad. The messier they did things, the more they laughed and enjoyed themselves at the housewife's expense. Needless to say, they got fired and kicked out of the house as soon as the lady got home from work. This is exactly what those girls wanted, and that is ex-

actly what they got. The angry and disappointed housewives who had been victimized lost no time telling the other ladies of the neighborhood about the terrible mess the Starting Supper girls had made, and warned against employing them.

These mean tricks might have worked in getting Cynthia a bad reputation except that one housewife called Cynthia directly to complain. Cynthia went over to her house and soon realized what her enemies were up to. She explained that it was not her girls who had made a mess in the kitchen, but a group of jealous girls who were out to discredit her. Cynthia got her school yearbook, and the angry housewife was able to pick out the girls from the pictures. Cynthia went to all the houses in the neighborhood, and soon everyone realized that Cynthia didn't do these bad stunts, and everyone cooperated in identifying the real perpetrators. The victims called the parents of the girls who had made the messes and complained. This made those parents so embarassed that they offered to pay for all the damages and make the girls pay them back out of their piggy bank savings. They were disappointed that their children could have been so mean as to instigate such unfair tricks.

Cynthia's dad was quite proud of the success of the Starting Supper crew. He was glad that they fought back when the trouble started. So that no one else would ever succeed in impersonating them, he took the girls to his office and had security identification tags made for each of Cynthia's employees. These had the girl's picture and name along with the Starting Supper emblem in a special laminated plastic covering. It is the same system that most businesses use to make sure that no unauthorized persons get into places that they don't belong. Cynthia told all her customers about the identification tags, and asked them to please not admit anyone into their homes who was not wearing one.

Cynthia was saving the money she earned for her future education. She planned to expand her operation to the adjacent neighborhood as soon as she could train a few of the girls with a culinary talent to take on some supervisory chores. She wrote in her junior high yearbook that she wished to be the owner of a famous restaurant when she grew up. No one had the slightest doubt that she would reach that goal.

THE COUNTRY CLUB

There are times when a kid wants to be with his friends, and just his friends. Brothers, sisters, cousins, aunts, uncles, and even parents can be a bother when a guy doesn't feel like playing the role of sibling, nephew, or son. It would be nice to have a place that was off limits to everyone except your best buddies. By off limits I mean that nobody even gets close. And this includes parents, teachers, salesmen, and especially other kids.

This is why we started the Country Club. The we I refer to is my fellow successful kids, successful in business. My name is Jonathan and I have a successful detective agency. It started out by my looking for lost pets and then evolved into a home-protection business where I do house sitting when people are away. It turns out that I often have money in my pocket while most of the other kids don't. They are always after me to spend my money and then give them some of whatever it is that I buy. I didn't mind sharing the first time or two, but it sure got to be a habit in a hurry. I would be the only one to pay, and never anyone else. It got me more and more annoyed, and soon I didn't find those kids much fun to be around anymore.

I found myself hanging around with Elizabeth and Donald. They started a Toy Store business. Their experience was much like mine. They were expected to pay all the time, and they always attracted a bunch of mooching kids whenever they went anywhere.

Then Cynthia joined our little circle. She had the successful Starting Supper business and found it agreeable to be with other kids who had found a way to get their own spending money. Also, we had a lot more to talk about, in that we were always trying to make our businesses go more efficiently, and found that kids who had their own businesses understood better and could often offer interesting suggestions.

We were soon joined by Gerald. He had started a pet boarding business and it was expanding all the time. He had built special kennels and compartments and kept people's pets while they were away.

Catherine and Diane had started a little business of giving horse-riding lessons. They are the girls who had found that valuable show horse and had gotten some riding horses as a reward. There were always things they needed for their horses and they hated to keep asking their parents. So they started out by giving an occasional riding lesson for fifty cents or so, and gradually built up a really profitable business teaching both Western and English riding to the kids who had either just gotten their own horse or wanted to learn to ride so that they could enjoy summer camp vacations more. When Catherine and Diane heard about our group of business oriented kids, they began hanging around with us more and more in their spare time.

Ronald wanted to join us without having a business of his own. His parents were quite wealthy and he never asked anyone to buy anything for him. We thought about it and decided that just having money wasn't the reason we were forming a club. It was the fun of associating with other kids with like interests who had achieved at some business. Isn't that the reason for clubs of any kind? It is the similarity of interests, whether it is the boy scouts, the 4 H, the Lion's club, the Rotary Club, and even the Masons. We hated to turn Ronald down, as he really is a nice guy. But Ronald had a lot of spunk and started a printing business. He got his parents to buy him a press and took it from there himself. He goes to the merchants and finds out what is on sale. Then he offers to print up little advertising handbills for them and distribute them around the neighborhood. It works out well as an economical way for the little shopkeeper to advertise, because usually he can't afford the prices that newspapers charge.

One of the more recent kids to join us is Lemuel. His mother is a widow and the family is poor and lives near the ghetto area of town. But he is ambitious and started a comic book exchange. He noted that most of the kids couldn't afford to buy many comics and so he got the idea of a lending library and book exchange business. You can rent a book for a penny a day. If you want to exchange some books, it is three of yours for two of his. He can't give an even exchange because then he would have no profit. His didn't make as much money at the other businesses, but he fulfilled the most important criterion for membership, which is ambition. He is already planning to get a small computer to keep track of his books and to expand to a city-wide operation and add employees. He will probably eventually have the most profitable business of any kid in the group, and he is willing to be patient and achieve his goal a small step at a time.

We had been meeting informally in each other's houses. But we were always being monitored by parents and siblings to some degree. We needed a place of our own, where just club members had access and anyone who was not a member could not get in. We found such a place at my Uncle Harry's. He is a bachelor. That means that he has no wife or children. He had bought an old house at the edge of town that was really too big for him. It was so cheap that he couldn't resist buying it. He said that we could use the cellar for our clubhouse. It fit our needs quite well. There is a basement door from the outside that can be separately locked. In this way we didn't track dirt through Uncle Harry's living room when we came and went. Daniel, the locksmith's son, had joined our group. His business was fixing locks by mail. He didn't want to compete with his dad, so he put an ad in the paper that he would fix any lock sent to him, and return it by mail. But most of his spare time was still spent in his dad's shop, where he did most of his work. He met the criterion of having his own business, and that was all that mattered to us. He was the one who installed the new lock on our clubhouse entrance and made and distributed the keys among the members.

We got to work and fixed up our clubhouse. We put in partitions so that we could have separate activity centers. We found that there was plenty of useful stuff in our parents' and grandparents' attics and garages. We soon had a ping-pong table set up. Another area was for watching T.V. on an old but perfectly useable set. We even got an excellent Hi-Fi when someone had to have the latest model, and gave away a perfectly good set to us kids because his trade-in allowance was so small that he would rather give it away than take such a small sum. We find this curious, that some people are never satisfied with what they have whenever something newer and fancier is available. Oh well, their loss is our gain.

The best thing we got was the refrigerator. Now we could keep all sorts of snacks in there. Cynthia kept it well stocked with whatever food she had left over from her catering business.

The one thing that was totally unexpected was the harassment from bullies. A group of bigger kids had their own club, which they called the Tough Guys' Club. I never had anything to do with them because all they were interested in doing was hanging around video arcades or looking for trouble. We all avoided them because they always wanted to borrow our bikes or baseball equipment

and then return it in damaged condition. It seems that there are kids who don't like it when they are excluded from anything, whether or not they earned the privilege of being included. The bullies were like this. Rather than build up something for themselves, they wanted us to open up our club facilities to them at no cost, or shut down. Of course, we refused to let them use our clubhouse. The bullies began to chase us. That was when I began to use my detective brain. We took to using disguises. If they couldn't recognize us, they couldn't follow and harass us. We even had special cloaks made that were the same color of bushes that we could put on so that we were harder to detect if they chased us into the woods. But the bullies knew where our clubhouse was, and they began to wait for us in the vicinity of Uncle Harry's house.

It was Uncle Harry who helped us solve this problem. He told us that there was a large, old abandoned sewer line that ran very close to the basement. He gave us the old maps, and we found it easy to make an opening from the basement into that sewer tunnel. It was dry and didn't even smell bad. The best part was that it was big enough for a kid to walk through standing up. We used the map, and found that we could follow the tunnel and emerge to the surface in a number of places that were in abandoned areas and were virtually undetectable. This really confused the bullies. They would watch us enter Uncle Harry's basement, but never saw us leave. They would just sit there and wait for us to come out. They would wait and wait, while we were really at home, laughing at their stupidity. Sometimes we would carry packages to the club house that we would purposely drop. They were like traps to get even with the bullies because they would explode with stinky perfume if anyone opened them. That sure made the bullies cautious about trying to grab things away from us. They soon gave up bothering us in the area of the clubhouse but harassed us whenever they met any of us on the street. We got to carrying walkie-talkie units so that we could summon help if we got into a tight situation. We had bought these radio units at a surplus store for a very cheap price, and they sure came in handy. It is typical of bullies to go around in gangs and pick on kids as individuals. They never want to get caught in an even situation where they might have to prove that they are really better. By calling for more kids, the threatened club member could usually get the bullies to go away without starting a fight that they knew they couldn't finish.

One day we went to the clubhouse and found that it had been broken into. Our padlock had been sawed off with a hacksaw. The place was left a shambles. What the burglars couldn't carry off, they wrecked. I found fingerprints all over the place, and they were the prints of kids, not the bigger fingerprints of adults. It was obviously the gang from the Tough Guys' Club that had wrecked our place. It was lucky for us that they didn't find our secret passageway, which had a fake wall in front of it. We thought of calling the police but decided to make sure of our suspicions first. I got my high-powered telescope from my house and went to the hill that overlooked the place where the bullies had their clubhouse. I could see them clearly, and they couldn't see me at all. Our suspicions were confirmed. They had all our stuff - our T.V., our Hi-Fi, our ping-pong table, our chairs, our dartboard, everything that was capable of being moved. It made me so angry that I wanted to hire some really big tough kids to go and beat all of them up. But that would have just made things worse, because they would do the same type of thing to us. I wanted to have an end to the bullies' harassment once and for all, rather than having to always waste time finding ways to cope with them.

Our members had a quick meeting, and we decided that the only really proper thing was to bring in the police. I called my friends at the police station and told them what happened. Boy, were the bullies surprised to see those squad cars pull up in front of their shack with me and the members of our club in the back seats. Luckily, we had proof that we owned all those things that the bullies had stolen from us. Also, the men in the police burglary division had gone to our club and gotten the bullies's fingerprints from the things they had wrecked and left behind. There was so much proof that the parents of the bullies made them plead guilty to theft, and paid us the money it would take to get our club fixed up again. The judge told the bullies that they were on probation, and that if they did anything like

this again, they would have to go to a special
school for juvenile delinquents.

I know it is mean to add punishment on to
punishment, but we just couldn't help getting in
our own little revenge. When the bullies weren't
in their clubhouse, we went there and did things
like pull out most of the nails that held their
shack together. The shack collapsed on them at
their next meeting, during a windstorm. The laugh
we got over that was the real compensation for all
the trouble they had caused us.

We found that our problems with bullies and
jealous people took care of itself as our
membership increased. Kids began to get ideas for
additional businesses, and we were adding new
members all the time. A girl started an escort
business with a bicycle built for two people to
ride at the same time. She had found the old
bicycle in the attic and had her dad fix it up.
Her business was to take kids to things that
didn't really need a parent, such as to the girl
scout meetings or to after-school activities.
Parents called her and she arranged a regular
schedule of pick-up and delivery. She did most of
the pedalling and didn't ask her passenger to help
unless they were going up a hill. Another kid
rented roller skates to teenagers and adults in
the parks on weekends. Two sisters started a
childrens' clothing exchange. They noted that
kids often outgrew clothing before it was worn
out, and they offered to buy such clothes or
exchange them for clothes that were of a larger
size. Of course, they had to profit on the ex-

change, especially since they took the trouble to wash and iron and repair any little defects in the clothes. Soon we weren't just an isolated group of a few kids, but had a membership so large that we could easily cope with threats from any potential bullies. If they didn't stop bothering us, we'd go after them as a gang and see how they liked to be picked on and harassed by a larger group. They got the message and quit bothering us once and for all. It seems that in unity there is strength.

We are outgrowing our basement facility. Daniel had installed better locks and a burglar-alarm system in case someone tries to break in again. Now we are making plans to have a real country club soon, something like adults have. We want our own swimming pool and maybe even a tennis court. Of course, we aren't going to buy those things. Our swimming pool will be a bend in the river and our tennis court will be a net across a little-used street. But we will have our own building and a fence around the property, and it will be for members only. After all, why should just adults have special places to go to be with the people they like? And if you are ever in my neighborhood, and have a business of your own, please stop in. Ambitious guests are always welcome.

Certificate of Award

This Certifies that

_____

has successfully completed
the Christman course in
PROGRESSIVE PHONICS

_____
Signature of Instructor